The Chittagong Hill Tracts

The Chittagong Hill Tracts
Militarization, oppression and the hill tribes

Anti-Slavery Society
Indigenous Peoples and Development Series
Report No. 2 — 1984

Published by Anti-Slavery Society
180 Brixton Road
London SW9 6AT

Typeset by Shanta Thawani
Printed by Whitstable Litho on 100% recycled paper

ISBN 0 900918 19 5

Rate of exchange: 36 takas to £1

Maps by Tessa Hearn
Cover photograph:
A Chakma mother from the hill tracts
Camera Press

Acknowledgements
Many people have contributed to this report. For their own safety –
particularly those living in Bangladesh and those who hope to return
there one day – they must regrettably remain anonymous. Compilation,
additional research and editing were carried out by Julian Burger and
Alan Whittaker of the Anti-Slavery Society, London.

Contents

Preface

It is routine, and recommended by the authorities, for foreign aid workers to travel with an armed guard in the Chittagong Hill Tracts district of Bangladesh. Early in 1984 three employees of the oil multinational, Shell, travelled without their escort and paid the penalty of being kidnapped and collectively offered for ransom.

Their kidnappers were the Shanti Bahini, the Peace Force, composed of men drawn from the 13 tribes of the hill tracts. These "miscreants" as the government in Dhaka calls them, are waging an armed and bloody war against the 30,000 Bangladeshi regular troops posted to the tracts. The Shanti Bahini maintain the fighting has been forced on them and is being carried out in defence of their land, homes and way of life. The government, anxious to modernise what it sees as a backward part of the country, has started a number of economic programmes in co-operation with international development agencies and has attracted 400,000 Bengalis into the area with promises of land and money.

The traditional inhabitants, the hillmen, are not Bengalis, and are not consulted by Dhaka. What the government sees as 'development' the tribespeople see as, at best, 'exploitation' but more commonly as ethnocide verging on genocide.

The conflict, in one form or another, has been fought for two decades, but its ferocity and seriousness have increased during the last five years. Bangladesh has taken not just the route of military dictatorship but has also oriented itself towards Islamic fundamentalism.

The hillmen are predominantly Buddhist and one of their leaders has declared that "if things continue as they are at the moment then in ten years time there will be no tribal people".

On 3 October 1980, the then Member of Parliament, Upendra Lal Chakma, who is the leading figure in the political life of the hill tracts, and a hillman himself, made it plain in a press release that

The tribal people of the Chittagong Hill Tracts are citizens of Bangladesh and they want to live with equal rights and status of citizens of Bangladesh. But if

7

Map 1 Bangladesh

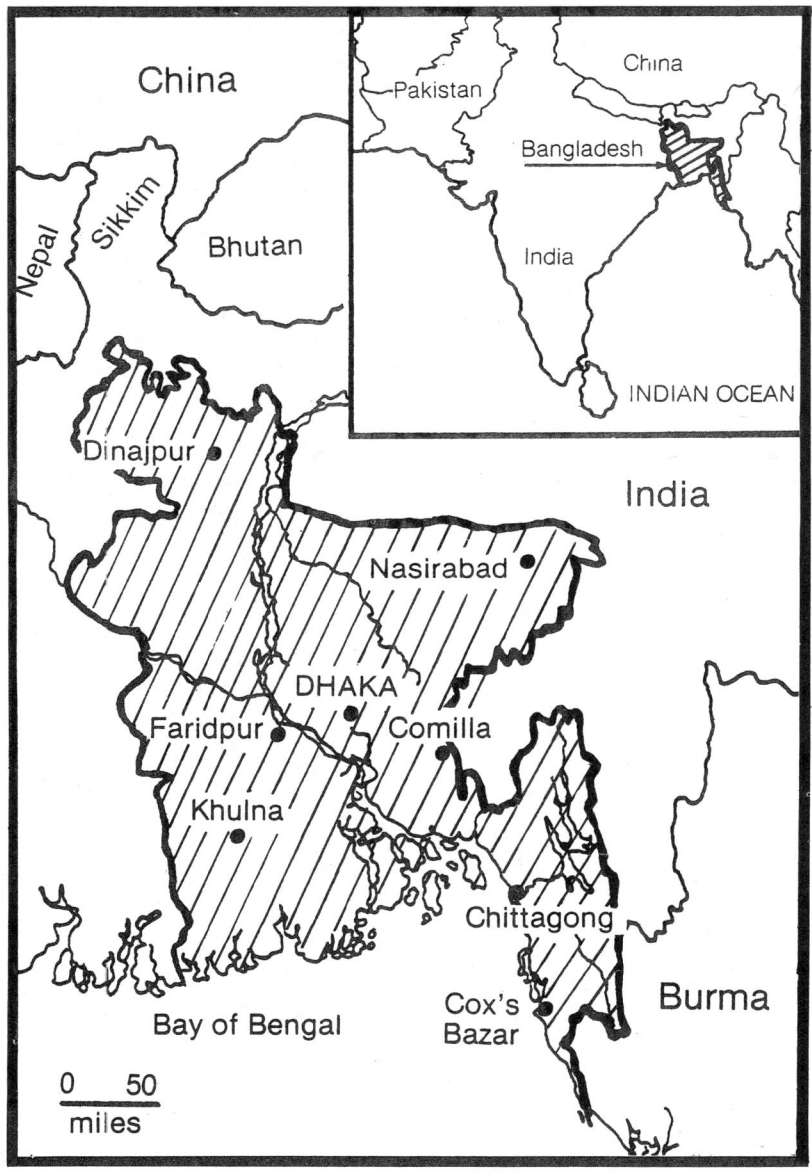

the government policy of oppression continues they will have to choose the path of violent movement for the restoration of their legitimate rights and the government shall have to bear the responsibilities for any untoward consequences.

Bangladesh is one of the poorest nations on earth. It is generally flat, subject to monsoon floodings and its population is growing at a yearly rate of 2 per cent which will result in a population of 128 million by the end of the century, according to Bangladesh's official *Statistical Yearbook, 1979.* With the exception of the city states of Hong Kong and Singapore, Bangladesh is the world's most densely populated country and the district around its capital, Dhaka, with over 2,600 people per square mile is the most densely populated of all.

In contrast, is the district of the Chittagong Hill Tracts. It is an upland area, forested and, with a hundred people a square mile, is the least densely populated district in the country.

It is this apparent emptiness, coupled with such factors as that nationally 77 per cent of the population work in agriculture, that have led to the conflict of interests, the clash of cultures and the murders, rapes and other atrocities that take place almost daily in the course of the undeclared war currently fought in the Chittagong Hill Tracts.

Map 2 Chittagong Hill Tracts

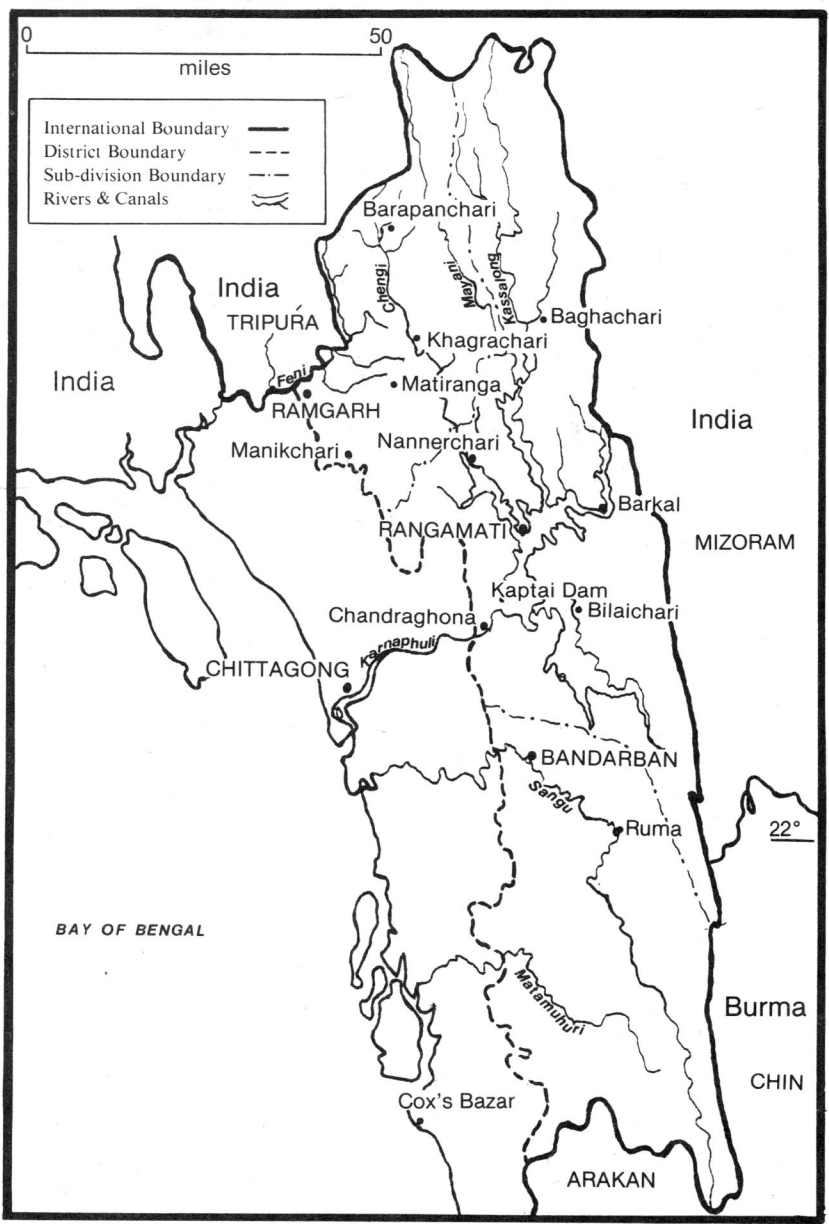

International Boundary
District Boundary
Sub-division Boundary
Rivers & Canals

India
TRIPURA

India

Barapanchari

Baghachari

Khagrachari

Matiranga

Feni

RAMGARH

Manikchari

Nannerchari

Barkal

RANGAMATI

India

MIZORAM

Kaptai Dam

Chandraghona

Bilaichari

CHITTAGONG

Karnaphuli

BANDARBAN

Sangu

Ruma

22°

BAY OF BENGAL

Burma

CHIN

Matamuhuri

Cox's Bazar

ARAKAN

Chapter One
The Tracts and their People

The Chittagong Hill Tracts have for centuries been remote and isolated from daily contact with the outside world. Today, they are designated an official administrative district of one of the newest of nations, Bangladesh. At 5,095 square miles, they form the country's largest district, accounting for about 10 per cent of its surface area. Its political, but not natural, boundaries are shaped by the Indian states of Tripura in the north and Mizoram in the east, by Burma in the south and east and, in the west, by the Chittagong District of Bangladesh. The tracts are made up of several valleys formed by the rivers Feni, Chengi, Mayani, Kassalong, Sangu, Matamuhuri and, most importantly, because of its contemporary industrial harnessing, the Karnaphuli. It is a largely inaccessible land of hills and ravines and cliffs blanketed originally in bush and creeper jungle. Its ridges reach heights of 3,000 feet, are covered in forests and run in a north-west/south-east direction.

Geographically, the district contrasts greatly with the alluvial, monsoon-flooded plains of the rest of Bangladesh.

The Chittagong Hill Tracts, until the 1970s, were inhabited by people numbering only 0.7 per cent of the total population. These, the 600,000 or so tribespeople, have traditionally made their homes in the tracts, identify themselves with pride as hillmen and historically have kept a distance between themselves and the majority population of Bangladesh, the Bengalis. They are of Sino-Tibetan descent, have a distinctive Burmese appearance and are short in stature. In physique, in religion, in lifestyle and, in some cases, in language, the hillmen are closely identified with their neighbours in north-east India and Burma.

The indigenous people of the Chittagong Hill Tracts contrast greatly with most of the people in the rest of Bangladesh.

Bengalis began to migrate in small numbers into the tracts during the 17th century. In the 1850s and 1860s the Chakma Raja, Dharam Bux Khan, and later his successor, Rani Kalindi, on the advice of the British and their own, few, Bengali officials, brought Bengali cultivators to work on the raja's land and to teach lowland farming to the Chakmas in general. During the 19th century only tribal chiefs were permitted to own land and the Bengali immigrants became sharecroppers. It was only later that some of them purchased land. Nevertheless, the Bengali population remained small and even by independence in 1947 it amounted to only about 2 per cent.

But after independence the Bengali population began to rise. By 1951 it was 9.1 per cent of the total; by 1961 it had become 17.7 per cent and in 1980 it had reached 27.5 per cent. Since the 1960s Bengali immigration has increased rapidly and this has created serious tensions with the original inhabitants.

The hill people are composed of 13 main tribes. The 350,000 Chakmas form the largest of these and they occupy the central and northern parts of the district, including its capital, Rangamati. The Marmas number about 140,000, live in the southern and north-eastern parts of the tracts and, like the Chakmas, are Buddhists. The 60,000 or so Tripuras practise a form of Hinduism, live mostly in the north and are related to similar peoples in the neighbouring Tripura state of India. Together these three tribes make up about 87 per cent of the hill peoples and, in contrast to the rest of the hillmen, live mainly in the valleys. The other tribes, numbering together about 40,000, live mostly in the south, occupying the forested hill ridges. They include the Tanchangya, Ryang, Murung, Chak, Khumi, Mro, Khyang, Bonjugi, Pankhu and Lushai peoples. The latter two tribes speak a language belonging to the Tibeto-Burmese group.

TABLE I

Population and Religion

Chakmas	Buddhist	350,000
Marmas	Buddhist	140,000
Tripuras	Hindu	60,000
Mros	Animist	5,000
Tanchangyas	Animist	
Ryangs	Animist	
Khumis	Animist	
Chaks	Buddhist	
Murungs	Buddhist	35,000
Khyangs	Buddhist	
Bunjugis	Christian	
Pankhus	Christian	
Lushais	Christian	
	Total	**590,000**

Map 3   Main Tribal Distribution in the Chittagong Hill Tracts

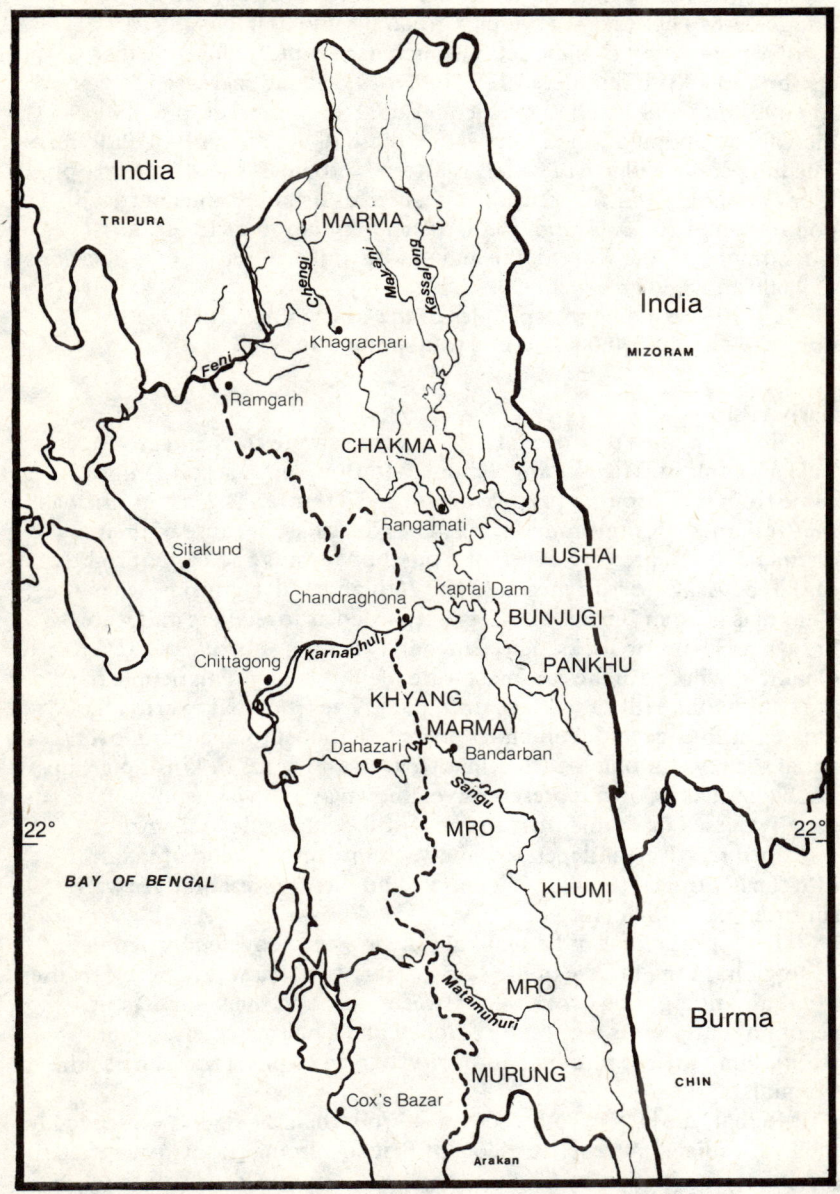

Two-thirds of the people of the hill tracts are Buddhist and under 20 per cent practise Islam, which is overwhelmingly the majority religion of Bangladesh. The rest are Hindus, Christians and animists.

The population of the tracts has increased rapidly since the turn of the century. In 1901 it numbered 125,000; in 1931 it had increased to just over 210,000 and by 1974 it had reached 508,000. However, despite the increase, the population density is one-tenth of the rest of Bangladesh. The hill people still live in widely scattered settlements and there are only four population centres officially classified as urban: Rangamati, with a population of 20,500; Bandarban, with a population of 13,500 and Chandraghona and Kaptai, the main industrial centres, with populations of 9,600 and 8,300 respectively.

In 1980, the indigenous peoples of the Chittagong Hill Tracts numbered about 590,000 out of a total population of 815,000.

Early History

The earliest people to move into the hill tracts were the Kuki group: Lushai, Pankhu, Mro, Kyang, Khumi and Bonjugi. A second migration came from the Tripura group: Murung and Tripura. The last group was the Arakanese: Ryang and Marma. The Chakmas, because of their distinct culture, are very different from the Marmas and cannot rightly be said to be Arakanese in origin. In the 16th and 17th centuries, when the Chakmas lived in Burma, they were regarded as foreigners and were known as Theks or Tseks. The Tanchangyas are a subtribe of the Chakmas who, with the Marmas, were the last Mongolian people to enter the Chittagong Hill Tracts a century later. The Chakmas exerted the greatest influence and their chiefs exercised almost total control over tribal society. Among the Chakmas there are 40 *gozas* or kinship groups. Each *goza* has its own representative, known as a *dewan,* whose office is usually passed on from father to son. Until British rule each *goza* remained relatively independent but with the introduction of taxation into the hill tracts, the Chakma people and their representatives were subordinate to their chief.

The coastal plains of Bengal have always been coveted by peoples of the region. In the middle of the 17th century the area was annexed by the Mughals and fighting broke out between them and the Chakmas. An accommodation was eventually reached and Chakma chiefs, while maintaining their traditional authority, agreed to pay a trade tax to the Mughals.

Mughal rule lasted from 1666 until 1760 when the region was ceded to the East India Company. Subsequent British administrators permitted the system of domination by Chakma chiefs to continue largely untouched until 1901, when they introduced the Hill Tracts Manual.

British Administration

The Bengali population, small though it was in the 19th century, exerted considerable influence on the local economy, and discontent among the tribespeople grew. As a result, the British authorities promulgated the Chittagong Hill Tracts Regulation of 1900, which provided for limited selfgovernment by the tribespeople. The regulation made it clear that:

> no person other than a Chakma, Mogh or a member of any hill tribe indigenous to the Chittagong Hill Tracts, the Lushai hills, the Arakan hill tracts or the state of Tripura shall enter or reside within the Chittagong Hill Tracts unless he is in possession of a permit granted by the Deputy Commissioner at his discretion.

Strict conditions attached to the regulation which made obtaining a permit almost impossible.

The 1900 Regulation divided the hill tracts into three revenue circles, each headed by a raja. The three circles, known as the Chakma (1,658 square miles) the Mong (653 square miles) and the Bohmong (1,444 square miles), together had representatives from all the tribes. These circles were in turn divided into 369 *mouzas,* each under a headman. The *mouzas* were made up of a number of villages with their own *karbaris,* the village leaders. The headmen of the *mouzas* were particularly influential and allocated land for shifting cultivation, collected revenue and settled disputes.

Various administrative changes were made under British rule. Under the 1900 Regulation the tribespeople administered the district although ultimate authority resided in a British–appointed deputy commissioner. In 1921, the regulation was amended to declare the Chittagong Hill Tracts a 'backward Tract' and gave the Governor-General-in-Council sole authority in the area. The 1935 Government of India Act created a totally 'excluded area' and so gave further recognition to the special status of the district. When the partition of the subcontinent was being discussed, the principal chiefs demanded status as a 'native state'. Later, they suggested a confederation with neighbouring Tripura, Cooch Behar and parts of Assam.

The Economy

Ninety per cent of the people in the tracts depend upon subsistence agriculture. The majority of these are involved in shifting cultivation which is known locally as *jhuming* and has been practised in the tracts since earliest times. The essentials of *jhum* cultivation are the clearing and burning of surface vegetation before planting mixed crops of rice, millet, sesame, maize, vegetables and cotton. The mixed nature of cropping ensures a supply of food for most of the year. At the end of an annual cycle the land is left to revert to scrub and the cultivators move on. The *dao,* or broadknife, is the main instrument used in clearing and planting.

For centuries *jhum* cultivation worked effectively. There was no serious deterioration of the soil and the plots lay fallow for at least seven years. This allowed regeneration of the soil and natural growth of the forest. Fallow periods are essential to *jhuming,* which is ecologically unharmful, but which also demands large areas per family as only part of the land is under cultivation at any one time. If either the population increases or the land decreases shifting cultivation is no longer viable.

Pressures on shifting cultivation in the hill tracts began in the 1860s. The British, with a view to protecting the watershed, banned it in the 1870s from some 800,000 acres – approximately one-quarter of all forest land. By reducing the area available for *jhuming,* the remaining land had to be used more frequently so soil deterioration set in. In 1959 work began on a massive hydro-electric project at Kaptai. On its completion in 1963 about 100,000 tribespeople were displaced. These were mainly sedentary rice farmers and many were forced into *jhum* cultivation and so added to the pressures.

During the last 50 years the fallow periods have become dangerously shortened. Less secondary growth has taken place and therefore less organic fertilizer, in the form of potash after burning, has been created. The nitrogen content of the soil has declined, as has crop yield. Shifting agriculture is no longer able to support the tribal population and the reduced fallow period has led to ecological deterioration. A century ago the Chittagong Hill Tracts were self-sufficient in food, but now they are not.

The hill slopes used for shifting cultivation traditionally belonged to tribal society as a whole. Tribesmen did not establish exclusive individual rights to any particular piece of land, only to the crops grown on their plots. Even today, in principle, any hillman may start *jhum* cultivation wherever he pleases. Tradition and practice give a *jhumia* prescriptive rights to his plot and first refusal of his old *jhum.* But in fact the circumstances of life in the tracts make this virtually impossible.

With the establishment of British control came state ownership of the land of the Chittagong Hill Tracts. Tribespeople were encouraged to become sedentary cultivators through the imposition of a *jhum* tax, which itself was a development of the poll tax paid to the chief from time immemorial. The hill slopes are still owned by the state, now Bangladesh, and they continue to be used for shifting cultivation. The village headman is responsible for the distribution of *jhum* land to villagers. The amount of land depends on family size and a rent is paid to the state through the headman. However, the authority of the village headman in these matters is now being superseded by the state administration.

While shifting cultivation is the predominant form of agriculture in the Chittagong Hill Tracts, some 100,000 acres along the river valley are used for intensive farming. In the valleys, farmers have land titles and are able to transfer land. Formal transfers can be done only with the deputy commissioner's permission on the recommendations of the headmen who, however, are being bypassed more and more. All grants of land to recent Bengali settlers have been made without the support of the headmen. The land in the valleys belongs to comparatively few owners who lease it out or use landless labourers to cultivate it for them. Rice is the major crop in this form of settled agriculture and it is supplemented by vegetables and pulses.

Only about 800,000 acres of land in the tracts are suitable for horticulture. The government has been attempting to introduce this more settled form of production but, in practice, inadequate marketing and poor roads have meant that farmers receive low incomes.

TABLE 2

Land Use

	Acres	Percentage
Land suitable for rice cultivation	77,000	2
Land suitable for horticulture and tree crops	670,000	21
Land suitable for forest only	1,600,000	51
Reserve forests	800,000	26
Total	**3,147,000**	

Based on Forestal's survey, 1964 to 1966

The 1900 Regulation was ambiguous on forest administration. The British recognized the importance of the huge timber resources of the area and sought to protect them for future exploitation. In 1928 the 1900 Regulation was amended and the hill tracts were divided into areas of forest reserves where no one was allowed either to live or grow crops. This prohibition adversely affected *jhum* cultivators by barring them from their traditional land.

Permanent settled farming depends primarily on the use of the plough and the first attempt to introduce it into the tracts, by the British in the 1860s, was unsuccessful. However, by the end of the 19th century the shortage of *jhuming* land and decreasing yields forced many tribespeople, particularly the Chakmas, Marmas and Tripuras living in the valleys, to

17

A Mro village

Photo: Wolfgang Mey

adopt plough cultivation. From then on, a dual agricultural economy began to develop.

Shifting cultivation did not require elaborate marketing because it was practised at subsistence level; borrowing and bartering were the supporting pillars of the *jhum* economy. After the adoption of the plough, an agricultural surplus was created. In a relatively short time rice production in particular proved to be very successful. In 1918 a government officer wrote

> There is no doubt that the economic position of the plough cultivator (in the Chittagong Hill Tracts) is better than in the most favoured districts of Bengal. In one mouza of Maischari in the Chengi valley, a mouza full of plough cultivators, I found the estimated stock of paddy in the village to be 24,000 mounds, averaging no less than 3,000 per family. [One mound is approximately 82 lbs.]

By the 1950s approximately half the tribespeople were growing rice in the valleys. However, there were no means of disposing of these products profitably.

Local markets sprang up in many places but mainly along the rivers. The first to be established were at Chandraghona and Rangamati in the early years of this century. In the southern parts of the tracts there were practically no markets until the 1940s and the people of this area depended on traders setting up temporary stalls along the riverbanks.

The markets were encouraged by the British and were monopolized by traders coming from the plains. As early as 1928 a survey, cited in the 1975 *Bangladesh District Gazetteer,* noted that

> all such trade as exists in the Chittagong Hill Tracts is almost entirely in the hands of Bengalis from Chittagong; sale of paddy and cotton, the marketing of forest produce is controlled by the financiers of the plains. There are very few hillmen with sufficient capital for trade of any kind as they have a natural prejudice against leaving their hills and busying themselves in the intricacies of commerce.

Sixty years later the position, if anything, is worse. On market days tribespeople sell their produce, usually vegetables, bamboo and fruit, to Bengali middlemen who fix the price and sell such goods as salt, cloth or cooking utensils at inflated rates. The plainsmen have a traditional expertise in trading, and the creation of the markets has not benefited the hill people.

The *District Census Report* of 1951 confirmed this Bengali dominance.

> The economic condition of the District is very unsatisfactory. Trade is entirely in the hands of outsiders. There are 66 bazars (markets) in this district and only a few shops belong to the tribesmen. The itinerant traders also are practically all Bengalis from the Chittagong District.

19

Since this was written three decades ago the only change has been for the worse. The threat to the livelihood of the hill people is continuing but it is now accompanied by a threat to their lives.

As M Q Zaman said in a seminar held at the University of Rajshahi, Bangladesh, from 28 to 30 March 1980, Bengalis now own

> the best agricultural land, hold top administrative, commercial and business positions. All shops in the bazar, (twice weekly market places) are run by Bengali businessmen and traders from outside districts of Bangladesh. Not a single hillman will be found throughout the hill tracts running any shops in the bazar.

An eyewitness account of current exploitation was sent to the Anti-Slavery Society by a Western national resident in the tracts. The Society feels unable to publish his name for his own safety.

> There is a hidden understanding among the Bengali businessmen that they will not buy vegetables, fruits, etcetera from the tribals above a certain fixed value, which is much lower than the market price. One day at a Bandarban bazar, ginger was sold to a shop by tribals for 5 takas per mound (82 lbs.), when the actual market price was 5 takas per seer (2 lbs.). It is hard to believe, but it is a fact. I went to the bazar myself and found that a tribal woman sold 100 lemons to a Bengali wholesale buyer for 20 takas. After five minutes the Bengali wholesale buyer sold these lemons for 75 takas to another Bengali businessman who came from Chittagong. Tribal people can only sell their vegetables to local Bengali businessmen. The businessmen who come from outside Bandarban cannot buy vegetables from the tribals directly.

Zaman emphasizes that time is running out if policies, deliberate or not, of ethnocide are to be successfully reversed.

> Twenty years ago tribals were literally lords of the land in the Chittagong Hill Tracts, free to live according to their traditional way of life with almost no interference. Within the last two well-remembered decades they have become not only a minority in their own ancient homeland, but a depressed and impoverished lower stratum, often the servants of those who have taken their lands. The hour is late, but still some land remains under the tenuous control of tribesmen. If the present policy continues of making previously inalienable land alienable, in another twenty years most of the best land in the Chittagong Hill Tracts will have passed out of tribal control. The region will have become a jumble of industrial plants and army camps, with tribesmen doing their best to hide from rich Bengalis and foreign tourists.

Chapter Two
Internal Colonization

For the first eight years of the newly-independent Pakistan, the 1900 Regulation remained untouched in practice and continued to be the bureaucrats' handbook. The Pakistani authorities had continued the employment of the British district commissioner who, with the three tribal chiefs, managed to defeat the first serious administrative threat to the hillmen. They persuaded central government in 1955 to oppose a plan to abolish the tracts' special status. However, other attacks on tribal institutions were successful and paramount among these was the disbanding of the indigenous police force and the scattering of its officers. Bengalis were brought in as replacements.

The military government of President Ayub Khan instituted a basic democracies system, a multi-tiered form of administration, and announced it as a way of bringing workable democracy to an illiterate population. The Basic Democracies Order was enforced in 1959 and, whatever its intention, its effect was to start the militarization of the Chittagong Hill Tracts.

A new constitution of Pakistan came into being in 1962 and further weakened the traditional power of the tribal leadership. Two years later, in 1964, President Ayub Khan abolished the special status of the Chittagong Hill Tracts altogether. Since then Regulation 1 of the 1900 Regulation – better known as the Hill Tracts Manual – has enjoyed a peculiar status. It is not recognised under the constitution, but it has never been annulled.

After a short civil war, the two wings of Pakistan broke up in 1971 into the present states of Pakistan in the west and Bangladesh in the east. The birth of the new state of Bangladesh initially brought no change in policy in the Chittagong Hill Tracts.

A divisional commissioner is based in the port of Chittagong. Responsible to him is a deputy commissioner based in the hill tracts town of Rangamati and his administrative district is divided into three sub-divisions with their headquarters at Rangamati, Khagrachari and

Bandarban. Each of these sub-divisions, is further divided into 16 *thanas*. Literally *thana* means a police station though it also denotes a territorial unit; *thanas* are composed of union councils and there are 47 of these in the hill tracts. Each is headed by a chairman. Almost all the senior administrative posts are held by Bengalis although the chairman of the union councils are usually tribespeople.

In practice, although both the tribal and governmental systems of administration co-exist, major decisions are taken by central government. Finances are administered by the deputy commissioner and this has inevitably weakened the traditional tribal system. The present militarization of the tracts has, of course, superimposed itself on the civilian administration to the further detriment of tribal organizations.

The collection of land rent was the main function of the tribal administrative structure established by the British prior to 1900. The administration's tribal officials ultimately became members of a privileged class which was favoured by the state and allowed to own land. All other land was owned by the state and farmers had to pay six rupees per year to the *mouza* headman who was also the tax collector. He paid three rupees eight annas to the chief for each family cultivating a *jhum*. The headman remitted one rupee four annas to the state and retained the rest for himself.

Before 1900 the chiefs exercised total criminal and civil powers. According to the new rules of 1900, customary tribal law and the lesser civil and criminal powers were left with the chiefs and headmen. These powers allowed the tribal leadership to settle land disputes and control social, religious and economic affairs. Until 1964 central government exercised minimal control over the tribal chiefs and their administration. After this date control passed out of the hands of tribal leaders. Most importantly, the constraints on outsiders settling in the area were completely abolished.

The constitution of Bangladesh, adopted in 1972, made no mention of any special status for the Chittagong Hill Tracts. Manobendra Narayan Larma, Member of Parliament for Chittagong Hill Tracts North, in protest, refused to endorse the constitution. Because the main provisions safeguarding tribal interests have been abrogated, government officials in the hill tracts now enjoy wide discretionary authority and constitutionally exercise more power in the district than their counterparts elsewhere in the country.

Power is concentrated in the hands of the deputy commissioner who, as in the rest of Bangladesh, is the administrative head of the district; in the hill tracts he is also the district magistrate and consequently responsible for law and order. Additionally, he is in charge of all branches of revenue collection and the co-ordinator of all development work as well as being chairman of the district council and of innumerable other official and semi-official organizations. His powers are virtually unlimited. Even the six sub-divisional officers have more power in the hill tracts than their equivalents elsewhere; they collect revenue and have absolute judicial powers in criminal and civil suits. Other important officials (that is, additional deputy commissioners and superintendents of police) have similarly wide powers. Despite official declarations that the maximum number of jobs in the administration will be given to hill peoples they hold only a few low grade positions.

The attack on the indigenous hill tracts people, implicit in the 1972 constitution, took shape in the following decade when the Chittagong Hill Tracts District was reduced in June 1981 by the creation of the District of Bandarban. This divided the tribal region and was seen as an attempt to undermine the unity of the tribespeople. The Chakmas were confined mainly in the north and the Marmas mostly in the south. In November 1983 a third district, Khagrachari, was formed. *Thanas* with a Muslim majority, in contrast to those with a tribal majority, were given increased funds.

Bengali Settlement
The abolition of special status in 1964 opened up the Chittagong Hill Tracts to outsiders. Bengali families started settling there in numbers large enough to alarm the tribespeople, who felt that it was official government policy to outnumber them on their own land. Grounds for this fear could be seen in the industries whose founding in the tracts coincided with the influx of Bengalis who were given preferential employment.

In contrast to the suspicion the tribespeople felt for the Bengalis of the Pakistani era, was their lack of opposition to the settlement, which also took place in the 1960s, of refugees from India.

Eight years after the creation of Bangladesh, President Ziaur Rahman presided at a secret, mid-1979 meeting during which it was decided to settle 30,000 Bengali families during the following year. The importance of the meeting was emphasized by the attendance of Deputy Prime Minister Jamaluddin, Home Minister Mustafizur Rahman, the commissioner of the Chittagong Division and the deputy commissioner of the Chittagong Hill Tracts. A sum of 60 million takas was allocated to the scheme, but the budget heading under which this state money was provided was not disclosed.

As a result of the meeting, implementation committees, made up of government officers and leading Bengali settlers, were formed at district and sub-divisional levels. The district commissioner headed the district committee and sub-divisional officers the sub-divisional committees.

The committees appointed agents from among the Bengali settlers and assigned them to contact landless Bengalis willing to settle in the tracts. These were not hard to find and from February 1980 truckloads of poor Bengali families poured into the hill tracts attracted by the government scheme to provide five acres of land, 3,600 takas and provisions to each new settler family. According to USAID in July 1980, the government decided to resettle 100,000 Bangladeshis from the plains in the hill tracts in the first phase of this scheme.

From the government's viewpoint the settlement plan was successful from the start. By 1980 the Feni valley which borders on Tripura contained about 18,000 Bengali families and roughly 1,500 hill families. There are now even fewer tribespeople left and those who remain are eager to leave. About 15,000 refugees from India were rehabilitated in the Kassalong valley by 1963 and although the tribespeople were willing to accept the Indian refugees, they vehemently opposed the Bengali wave of settlement which began the following year.

Myani valley in the northern part of the district contains 40,000 indigenous people and about 10,000 Bengalis, a large number of whom arrived in the valley in 1980. In Chengi valley the Bengali settlements received 1,500 families between 1978 and 1980. By the same date there were 1,000 Bengali families at Kaptai and 5,000 families in Rangamati sub-division, of which, 3,500 families alone settled at Kalampati.

In the southern part of the district, the Lama *thana* has about 3,000 Bengali families and even more were settled at Nakyangchari. In Rangamati town, in 1980, hillmen accounted for about 30 per cent of the population.

In May 1980 the government confirmed its policy towards the Chittagong Hill Tracts and started actively to encourage settlers to move there. A secret memorandum (Appendix 1) from the commissioner of the Chittagong division to government officials in other districts stated that it was "the desire of the government that the concerned deputy commissioners will give top priority to this work and make the programme a success".

During 1980 some 25,000 Bengali families were settled in the hill tracts. At the same time thousands of tribal families, dispossessed by the Kaptai dam project in the early 1960s, were still attempting to get some kind of monetary or land compensation.

Under the second phase of the plan each landless settler family received five acres of hill land or four acres of mixed land or 2.5 acres of wet rice land. They also received two initial grants of 700 takas altogether, followed by 200 takas per month for five months and 12 *seers* (about 24 lbs.) of wheat per week for six months.

A Marma temple

Photo: Wolfgang Mey

By 1981 Bengalis made up nearly one-third of the total population of the hill tracts.

The Chakma leader, Raja Devashish Roy is on record as saying in 1981 that he had no prior knowledge about the settlement of Bengalis. He emphasized:

> I do not want settlers from outside the Chittagong Hill Tracts. The headmen are also against it. I have asked the government not to settle Bengalis in the district. Those who settle here are creating conflict with the tribal people ... Many are compelled to leave their ancestral homelands, some even going to India.

In July 1982 a third phase of Bengali settlement was authorised under which a further 250,000 Bengalis are expected to be transferred to the area.

Bengali settlers, with the connivance of the almost totally Bengali administration, have been able to take over land and even whole villages. There is severe population pressure on land in Bangladesh generally and tribal land has been regarded as readily available. One excuse often given for allowing or encouraging this immigration is the relatively low population density in the tracts. The United States Agency for International Development (USAID) has noted that "the Chittagong Hill Tracts are relatively less crowded than the plains of Bangladesh. Because of this difference in population densities, there has for some time been a migration from the crowded plains to the hills".

A study commissioned by Dhaka, however, concluded in 1967 that "as far as its developed resources are concerned, the hill tracts is as constrained as the most thickly populated district ... The emptiness of the hill tracts, therefore, is a myth".

Only five per cent of land outside forest reserves is suitable for intensive field cropping.

In spite of the shortage of farming land in the tracts, the government has succeeded in attracting many thousands of landless Bengalis. To be landless in Bangladesh is to be absolutely poor and dependent. Jobs are seasonal, insecure, and pay is enough for subsistence only. An agricultural labourer receives about five rupees a day when he is working and is usually unemployed for about six months of the year. For the overwhelming majority of Bangladesh's rural population there is little hope of escape from constant poverty. The settlement plans offer an opportunity which no landless or poor Bengali family can ignore. The land, however uncultivable, and the money and food grants, however, depleted by corrupt officials, can mean survival for six months or more for poor Bangladeshi peasants.

26

The Bengali peasants who move to the Chittagong Hill Tracts come principally from the plains districts of Chittagong, Noakhali, Sylhet and Comilla, and have no experience of hill slope cultivation. In order to avoid returning to the kind of exploitation they received at the hands of moneylenders and landlords they encroach on tribal-owned wet-rice land when they find they cannot make a living from the land they have been given.

Landlessness is on the increase in the country in general. Agricultural wages and *per capita* consumption of basic foodstuffs declined in real terms in the late 1970s. Land ownership has become increasingly concentrated and now 10 per cent of the population owns half the land. The poor – Bengalis and hillmen – are vulnerable and their poverty leads them into a dependent relationship with those who exploit them most. Rich farmers, village union chairmen and moneylenders are often the same people and they ensure that the benefits of any project designed to help the poor accrue to themselves. In the tracts, as in the rest of Bangladesh, these people are Bengali.

There has been no will on the part of any Bangladeshi government to assist landless labourers or marginal farmers anywhere in the country. Indeed organizations of landless people are often put down with the utmost brutality by hoodlums hired by local landlords, the police, the army, or by all three. The government's power rests with the middle and upper classes in the urban areas and with rich farmers. Since the foundation of Bangladesh there have been two five year plans emphasizing the need for land reform but no government has attempted to implement them. The Bengali poor will seize any survival chance they are presented with. Illiterates have limited horizons and they are not fully aware that the government's scheme to settle them in the Chittagong Hill Tracts is not essentially an attempt to improve their lot. It is a political act to nullify the question of tribal rights to self-determination by increasing the number of Bengalis in the hill tracts to a majority.

The Pakistani government instituted a settlement plan in the Feni valley bordering India because it distrusted the tribespeople living there. Bangladeshi governments have similarly used poor Bengalis against the hill people. There seems to be a determination to destroy tribal society and, if necessary, the tribespeople. Illiterate Bengali peasants who, under this scheme move to the hill tracts, know nothing of the tribal situation. All they know is that the government has given them land and is prepared to assist or at least to turn a blind eye to encroachment on tribal land.

As we have seen, the plan benefits rich farmers from the plains. Each family wanting to settle in the hill tracts needs a certificate from the union chairman, usually a rich farmer.

In many cases, it has been reported that instead of selecting landless peasants, the UP chairman selects marginal farmers and comes to a deal with them. The deal is – writing off the marginal farmer's land in favour of the chairman in exchange for the certificate.

Like so many projects in Bangladesh which claim to help the poor, the real beneficiaries are the rich.

The current government argument is that settlement in the hill tracts is necessary because much of the land there is uncultivated and therefore in their view wasted. Furthermore Dhaka maintains that "it would be against the Constitution to prevent any Bangladeshi from settling or buying land in any part of the country". This argument takes little account of the economic or political realities of the Chittagong Hill Tracts where little of the land is suitable for farming and where the traditional owners are coerced into giving up their property.

The 1976 Asian Development Bank (ADB) reported that "if the bumpy land were declared open to Bengali migrants, they would develop the more undulating parts into irrigated rice land in no time". However, by 1984 the region showed little evidence of economic improvement. The new Bengali settlers found it hard to farm tracts land successfully and this failure was quickly seen by Bengali entrepreneurs as an opportunity to make money for themselves. They persuaded the government to provide them with land, anything from 25 to 5,000 acres, and capital for the 'development' of the region. This has resulted in the usual Bangladeshi pattern: the rich get richer by exploiting the vulnerable.

A direct result of the settlement scheme works to the wider political advantage of Dhaka. The conflict between poor Bengalis and the tribespeople for a tiny proportion of the total land distracts attention from the general situation of landlessness in Bangladesh. In the hill tracts, this struggle has polarised the two communities. Bengalis, in collaboration with the army and police, harrass the hillmen. Civil suits taken out by tribal people have increased substantially but, since the judiciary is manned mainly by Bengali officials, they have been unsuccessful. Resulting from this, tribal families have been forced to leave their homesteads and become landless jhum cultivators.

In June 1981 the *Far Eastern Economic Review* reported that President Ziaur Rahman "... frankly admitted that the Dhaka authorities were planning to settle between 200,000 and 300,000 Bengalis in the Chittagong Hill Tracts area". The article continued by saying that Major General Manzur (GOC Chittagong – since killed by the army following the 1981 coup attempt) who was officially in command of the operations "is reported to have told acquaintances that he found them distasteful and that the Bengalis had begun to treat the Chakmas as badly as the Punjabis had once treated them".

Under Ziaur Rahman administrators of the settlement programme affected to know little about unofficial Bengali intrusion into the tracts. However, government officials maintain close contact with Bengali social welfare organizations which appear to have two main functions: to organize new batches of settlers, who are usually relatives and friends, and to harrass tribespeople so that they are compelled to leave the area.

Coup

In May 1981 President Ziaur Rahman was assassinated. Before presidential elections were held the army Chief of Staff, Lieutenant-General Mohammed Ershad, stated that the only president acceptable to the army would be Justice Abdus Sattar and insisted that the army should have a substantial say in governing the country. In November, Sattar was duly elected; but only four months later Ershad staged a bloodless coup, instituted martial law and suspended the constitution. Under martial law regulations political activity was banned and criticism of martial law became punishable with seven years' hard labour.

In October 1982, the government announced a new education policy which included the teaching of Arabic in Bangladesh's primary schools. This was seen as a step towards making the country into an Islamic state, a choice which had been rejected after the liberation war. It led directly to a series of demonstrations throughout the country. The government's response was to arrest between 1,300 and 3,500 people, including leaders of political parties, and to close all the universities in February 1983. Most detainees were released after a few days.

Education is seen not only as a means of Islamising what has been a secular nation, but also as a tool in reinforcing Dhaka's control over the Chittagong Hill Tracts. The hillmen had used education during the British colonial period as a way of asserting individual independence and of limiting the powers of the chiefs and *dewans* over them. Those who successfully finished their education obtained positions in the local administration. Today, education may be regarded as a means of repression.

In 1979 the National Foundation for Research on Human Resource Development found that fewer children completed their primary education in the Chittagong Hill Tracts than in any other part of Bangladesh. The principal reason for this must be the fact that teaching is done in Bengali – at best a second language for the hillchildren. The Chakmas, Moghs and Tripuras have their own written languages and each of the tract's thirteen tribes has its own language or dialect, neither of which is Bengali.

The government's insistence on overriding the linguistic requirements of the tribespeople contrasts with its policy overseas. In London, on 1

October 1983, the Bangladeshi High Commissioner addressed a seminar on the educational needs of Bangladeshis in Britain. He stressed that they have a deep attachment to Bengali and this is deep-rooted in "our history, tradition, culture and religion".

Two days later, on 3 October, General Ershad told a public gathering in Rangamati that the Chittagong Hill Tracts were to be developed as a 'special economic zone'. The government, he said, had prepared a special five year plan for the tracts and, as part of this, intended to set up between three and five residential schools in each district. He did not say why the schools had to be residential or if the teaching would be in tribal languages. He did say, however, that a total of 60 places would be reserved for the older children of tribespeople in medical, engineering, agricultural and cadet colleges and in polytechnics. In the tracts 'capital' of Rangamati 20 per cent of the places had been reserved for hill children in the paramedical institute.

The dominance of right wing fundamentalist Muslims in the Bangladeshi government and armed forces is increasing. Most of those in senior positions who actually fought for the liberation of Bangladesh have now been assassinated or edged from power. Given these changes and the continued insecurity of the government in Bangladesh it is likely that the tribal people will have to face even harsher attacks on their lands and culture in the future. The fundamental Islamic orientation of General Ershad is unlikely to be sympathetic to religious or other minorities.

The Dutch organization, International Fellowship of Reconciliation, in March 1983 stated that the government had made a secret plan to force tribespeople to embrace Islam and to this end soldiers stationed in the hill tracts were encouraged to marry tribal girls. The government had also received funds from Saudi Arabia to build a mosque and an Islamic Cultural Centre in Rangamati.

In the short period since the coup of September 1981, Ershad has concentrated state powers in his own hands. He is chief martial law administrator, chief of army staff, defence minister, commander-in-chief of the armed forces and president of the council of ministers. On 11 December 1983 he declared himself president.

But perhaps there is still a little hope for the future wellbeing of the people of the hill tracts – that is if Dhaka practises what it preaches.

At the Fourteenth Islamic Conference of Foreign Ministers held in the Bangladeshi capital, according to *Bangladesh Today* of 31 January 1984, agreement was reached on a Declaration of Human Rights in Islam. The hillmen will note the following extract:

> (we) believe in fulfilling the injunctions of the unchanging Islamic Shari'ah which calls for the safeguarding of man's religion, soul, mind, honour, wealth

and progeny, and which is universal in its applicability and is characterised by moderation in all its principles and rulings, which combines spirit with matter, and which balances individual rights and obligations and collective privileges, harmonises reason and emotion, idealism and reality, which guarantees justice to opponents in a manner that does not result in oppression or frustration.

General Ershad postponed the first elections to be held in 460 rural districts only six days before they were due to take place. This was regarded as a major concession by the opposition parties who had called for a boycott of the polls.

The planned election day, 24 March 1984, was significant: the second anniversary of Ershad's seizure of power.

Before the postponement was made public, Sheikh Hasina, the daughter of Bangladesh's first president, Sheikh Mujibur Rahman, told the *Guardian* newspaper (19 March 1984) that:

The army capture power first by the gun, then they indulge in politics. They form their own so-called parties, using the government's machinery and funds. They want to legitimise their power before the world.

When it announced the postponement of the rural elections the Ershad government said it had been done

to pave the way for national unity, dialogue and understanding for reaching the ultimate objective of transition to democracy by maintaining a peaceful atmosphere.

The last eight words of the statement in particular will be remembered by the people of the 13 tribes of the Chittagong Hill Tracts.

Chapter Three
Developing Poverty

By the 1950s the industrial capacity of both wings of Pakistan was concentrated in the hands of 43 families living in West Pakistan and owning three-quarters of the country's manufacturing assets. Economic decisions affecting the lives of millions of Bengalis were taken over 1,000 miles away in Karachi, Lahore and Rawalpindi. One of these decisions was to build the Kaptai dam.

Kaptai Dam
The dam was built across the Karnaphuli river near the hamlet of Kaptai, deep in the tribal territory of the Chittagong Hill Tracts. Construction of the dam began in 1959 and was completed in 1963. It was funded by a bilateral loan from the United States Agency for International Development (USAID).

The reservoir created by the hydro-electric project submerged 250 square miles of prime agricultural land making up 40 per cent of the total cultivable land in the tracts. Some 100,000 tribespeople, mainly Chakmas, were displaced by the project. These people, one-sixth of the total tribal population, were promised both financial compensation and substitute land. However, 60,000 received no compensation of any kind and about 10,000 migrated to India. Because they had no recognized land rights, no provision was made for those 8,000 *jhumia* families who had farmed the hillsides before they were flooded. These families were simply ignored, as indeed were the various communities isolated on small islands created by the lake. These, unable to continue farming, also joined the numbers dislocated by the dam.

The immediate consequence of the mass upheaval of the hillmen was that – simply in order to survive – many of them were forced into shifting agriculture despite the already severe shortage of *jhum* land in the tracts.

The average land holding of each of the 10,000 families with land rights in the valleys before they were flooded had been about six acres.

Approximately three acres of new land of comparable quality was made available to those tribal people lucky enough to receive any compensation. For this purpose a portion of the Kassalong reserved forest was used. Bengali settlers were the first to receive compensation.

A board of Revenue Compensation Office was established at Kaptai before the hydro-electric project was completed and, between 1959 and 1967, it disbursed 43 million takas, about £1.1m. In 1980, the *Far Eastern Economic Review* noted that of the $51 million set aside by the government for rehabilitation, only $2.6 million had actually been spent.

No social impact study was commissioned prior to the construction of the dam. Three years after the project was completed the Canadian company, Forestal Incorporated, was commissioned to study possible future developments in the hill tracts and the effect of the dam on the tribal society. Forestal found that before the dam was built: "The tribal people had attained a reasonably satisfactory way of life adequately adjusted to the limitations imposed by the physical environment". After the dislocation, however, the company reported that a disastrous cycle of over-cultivation had led to depletion of soil fertility, loss of forest cover, serious erosion and further increased pressure on the remaining land.

The 11-man team of geologists, economists, agronomists and biologists made two main recommendations. They proposed that *jhuming* should be controlled and that new horticultural production be introduced. The report came out strongly against shifting cultivation on the grounds that it could not achieve the productivity possible with modern sedentary farming methods.

Under the Pilot Scheme for the Control of Jhuming five *mouzas* covering over 35,000 acres were designated a Protected Area and forbidden to shifting cultivators. This land was to be planted with soft woods and fruit trees. However the programme was a failure and only 2,000 acres of fruit trees were planted.

The Standard Agricultural Holdings Program aimed at a major transformation of the hill tracts into an area of fruit production. It was due to be implemented in rehabilitation areas where dispossessed tribal families were being settled. Poor planning and administration was responsible for its failure. However, there was a more serious consequence as Wolfgang Mey pointed out at a conference at the University of Copenhagen in April 1983.

> Rice production was given up entirely in favour of fruit production. This meant the withdrawal of a sound economic basis of the concerned villages and the integration of nearly self-sufficient groups into the Bengali market economy. The results soon came. As people were compelled to work in these fruit gardens, they had no time to work in the swidden fields. Shortly afterwards lack of foodstuffs was reported, then the first cases of starvation.

Tribal settlers were unwilling to remain and today the *mouzas* where this programme was initiated are practically deserted.

Mey continues:

> Chakma peasants were compelled to render unpaid labour in the forests and in the settlements of the Forest Department's personnel; they were forced to buy in special shops whose Bengali owners had come to some profitable agreement with the Department's staff. Those Chakmas who resisted these practices were publicly beaten up, arrested and handed over to the Rangamati jail.

In 1966 Forestal also recommended the introduction of mixed plantation farming and although an attempt was made by the Board of Revenue Office at Kaptai to carry this out it was, according to John McKinnon's 1976 report, *Socio-Economic Aspects,* produced for the Asian Development Bank

> ... hurried, over-ambitious and many who had been resettled abandoned the land they had helped plant and retreated into the hills. According to the project director, no solely domestic food crops were included as part of the development programme. (Dr A H M Attaf Ali.) Farmers were dependent upon government support and if this was unreliable, farmers can hardly be blamed for falling back on their own resources.

Such plantation farming depended heavily on bringing fertilizers and pesticides into the tracts. It was usual for local government officers, always Bengalis, to steal these essentials and sell them on the black market.

Marketing was controlled by Bengali middlemen in league with local officials and the hillmen were always paid well below the market value for their plantation products. For example, a pineapple bought for 0.25 taka might sell in Chittagong, 50 miles away, for five takas, so giving the middleman a profit of 2,000 per cent.

Over-cultivation, as is evident from a glance at the landscape, led to erosion and to severe ecological damage. Hillsides are scarred by slips and the steep slopes are covered with scrub. Soil washed off the hills is said to form up to nine inches of sediment in a year in the shallow parts of the lake. The former *jhuming* cycle of ten to fifteen years, allowed forest regeneration but, so great is the pressure on land, this has now been reduced to two or three year cycles. In subsequent government and other reports the problem of ecological destruction is blamed on the primitive form of agriculture, that is, on *jhuming* rather than on the sudden reductions in land area available to shifting cultivators.

In 1976 the Asian Development Bank reported that one-third or more of all occupied land had been burnt off in preparation for planting. It unequivocably stated that:

The sociological impact of this ecological deterioration is indicated by the number of people dependent on government welfare measures (food-for-work) and the number of households prepared to enter government re-settlement schemes even where it is known that in the past these have largely failed.

It is certain that the dam caused immense human suffering; it is uncertain whether it has made a significant contribution to the economy of Bangladesh. The Kaptai dam and the Karnaphuli reservoir were and still are a significant source of electrical power. According to the Bangladesh Power Development Board in 1980, out of an installed capacity of 789 megawatts in the country, the Kaptai project provided 78 megawatts. However, this is only 0.5 per cent of the country's total energy supply and only 3 per cent of its commercial and industrial energy needs. The eastern electricity zone, in which the Kaptai dam is located, has major alternative sources of energy including both natural gas and oil deposits. Gas is already tapped and makes a much larger contribution to energy requirements. Recently-discovered oil deposits have not been developed due to lack of capital. The World Bank has refused to provide such capital, arguing that the Bangladeshi government should provide more incentives to attract investment from international oil companies.

Virtually all the electricity from the Kaptai project is supplied to urban centres outside the tracts. Even by 1983, Kaptai, Rangamati and Chandraghona were still the only hill towns receiving their power from the Kaptai project. Fewer than 10 per cent of the tribespeople live in these towns. Marischya, Khagrachari and other towns are fed by kerosene or diesel-powered generators and electricity is only available in government offices, police stations and military barracks. The vast majority of tribespeople have no electricity and are unable to afford it in any case, a condition they share with the majority of Bengalis.

The tribespeople have not benefited from the hydro-electric project and a majority of Chakmas feel it has made their life worse. A survey, published by Chittagong University in 1979 and carried out among the Chakmas by R I Choudhury and his colleagues found 69 per cent felt the dam created food and financial problems for them, 89 per cent said that they had to change residence due to inundation, 87 per cent faced problems due to change of residence, 69 per cent complained of inadequate government help for resettlement, 58 per cent were distressed that they had no scope for employment on the Kaptai hydro-electric project and 93 per cent felt that the economic condition of tribal people had been better before the Kaptai dam.

The Pakistani regime declared the hill tracts a tax-free area to facilitate development, companies were encouraged to exploit the area's resources and a few new industries were set up. The Karnaphuli paper mill was the largest of these and others were rayon, match and cigarette factories. Few benefits from these developments reach the tribespeople: for instance only about 40 hillmen are part of the Karnaphuli paper mill's 6,000 workforce. *The Economic and Political Weekly,* on 19 April 1978, stated:

> The industries and factories in the Chittagong Hill tracts do not benefit the tribal people as all employment goes to the Bengalis. More factories and industries mean more jobs for the Bengalis, and more hardship to the hill people.

The reservoir could have brought some benefits to the tribespeople by providing fishing but the centrally-administered Department of Fisheries controls marketing of the catch to the detriment of the tribal fisherman. The 1976 ADB report noted that the fishermen receive a very small proportion of the final retail prices: fish sold for 0.65 taka a kilo, was sold by the wholesaler for 2 takas and reached 15 takas in the urban markets.

In 1976 during his fact-finding mission to the Chittagong Hill Tracts, Major General Ziaur Rahman received a memorandum drawn up by the hillmen who told him that:

> The vast expanse of water captured by the dam provides a scene which impresses every visitor with its beauty. But could anybody have thought that this immense body of water is to some extent filled with the tears of the local people? Through the cables of the electric line not only current flows but also the sighs of grief.

Development in the Hill Tracts

The Chittagong Hill Tracts Development Board was created in January 1976. Although 60 per cent of the Board is made up of hillmen, control is in the hands of the government's Cabinet Division which is in charge of the general administration of the country. Muhammad M Huq in his study of the hill tracts remarks that:

> Real authority lies with the Cabinet Division at the Central Secretariat ... Even if the tribal component of the Board's personnel were 100 per cent instead of the present 60 per cent and the tribal representatives were in the majority in the consultative committee the situation could not have changed substantially.

The Chakma and Mong chiefs and other prominent tribespeople who are members of the Chittagong Hill Tracts Development Board have not been attending the board meetings during recent years in protest against its undemocratic structure. Indeed, since 1976 tribal chiefs have received a mere 1,000 takas and the *mouza* headmen only 300 takas monthly towards office maintenance. This is the only governmental allowance given them.

During its first three years the development board spent 93 million takas (£2.5m) on agriculture, transport, education, sports, culture, social welfare and health. Since its foundation, the board has also been responsible for the settlement of tribespeople displaced by the dam, and it initiated the joing farming scheme *(joutha khamar)* in order to settle the *jhumias.*

Much of the money for these projects has come from outside Bangladesh. Tribespeople are generally extremely suspicious of development projects because previous external involvement in the hill tracts has been detrimental. The creation of the forest reserves by the British, the building of the Kaptai dam by the Pakistani government and the massive Bengali immigration supported by the Bangladeshi government, have all robbed the tribespeople of this patrimony.

The Chittagong Hill Tracts Development Board, with the support of the Asian Development Bank, also plans to increase cotton yields massively to about 25,000 bales a year. The raw cotton produced would be of a high quality and too expensive for processing locally; it is much more likely to be shipped to Japan and so provide jobs there rather than in the tracts.

Development projects in the Chittagong Hill Tracts have been financed bilaterally by Sweden and Australia and by the multilateral agencies, the United Nations Children's Fund (UNICEF), the World Health Organization (WHO) and by the Asian Development Bank (ADB). The most destructive of these projects as far as tribal society is concerned are the forestry programme financed by the Swedish International Development Authority (SIDA) and the road building carried out by the Australian Development Assistance Bureau (ADAB). Official tribal representations, threats from resistance groups and protests from international human rights bodies (including the Anti-Slavery Society) led eventually to the withdrawal of both SIDA and ADAB before they had completed their projects.

Forests

Shifting cultivation is often blamed for the destruction of forests and in the hill tracts the *jhumias* have been accused of being solely responsible. However successive governments have themselves planned the ruthless felling of thousands of acres of forests.

Forests outside the tracts were cut down for firewood during the 1960s population boom. In 1965, the Bangladesh Forests Industries Development Corporation set up timber and furniture industries and planned to extract 45,000 tons of timber annually. In the same year coal imports from India were stopped and, as a result, yet further pressure was put on forest reserves throughout the country. This led to a tripling of market prices from 1970.

Until 1981, the Swedish International Development Authority (SIDA) was involved in a £6 million project to plant trees and provide technical training to tribespeople in forest industries and in road development. This project was part of a much larger afforestation programme which involved the planting during a period of 20 years of about 1,000 square miles of seedlings – amounting to 20 per cent of unclassed state forest. This massive commercial forestry programme would have led to the *jhumias* eventually being deprived of more than half their traditional land. For the tribespeople only the *joutha khamars* were left in the hill tracts.

In October 1981 SIDA stated that:

> Due to the political situation in the Chittagong Hill Tracts and the policies pursued by the Bangladesh Government ... the Swedish Government decided in 1976 not to continue to support the programme after its termination in June 1981. Such extension of project agreements are usually quite common. The main reason for the decision was the inability to give the programme such a direction as to benefit the ethnic minorities in the area.

Despite the diplomatic language there can be no doubt that SIDA was responding to a vigorous campaign in the Swedish press which had exposed human rights abuses by both the Bangladeshi government and army against tribespeople. The press also highlighted Sweden's assistance to the government and armed forces in the hill tracts including the army's use on the Kaptai lake of 10 fast Swedish motor launches, originally provided for the use of project workers.

Roads

In 1977 a feasability study for further developments in the hill tracts was commissioned from the West German firm of AUH in co-operation with Halcrow Fox and Associates, UK.

To make full commercial use of the forests, particularly during the rainy season, it is necessary to have good all-weather roads. The Australian Development Assistance Bureau undertook a road building programme to connect Khagrachari, located in the centre of the Chengi valley, with Rangamati 41 miles away, and to upgrade the Chittagong-Rangamati road. The Australian firms, McDonnel Gavin & Co and the Snowy Mountain Engineering Corporation, were contracted to survey and carry out construction work.

ADAB was also to plan roads which would improve access to the north, where two-thirds of the district's population live, and where three-quarters of the best agricultural land and the largest reserve forest, Kassalong, are located. Kassalong's 406,542 acres make up half the reserve forest in the hill tracts.

International aid donors and the Bangladeshi government argue that the new roads will improve the hill peoples' access to markets and will reduce their cultural and economic isolation. But in the past the relative inaccessibility of most of the area has been the predominant factor in maintaining tribal identity. As marketing is monopolised by immigrant Bengalis they will inevitably be the major, if not sole, beneficiaries of the road building programmes. The tribespeople's main worry is that the roads will increase the ease with which Bengalis can move into the area and take over ancestral tribal land and villages. The Australian organization, Community Aid Abroad, noted in 1981 that "the Chittagong Hill Tracts stands out as almost certainly the most destructive use of Australian aid anywhere in the world".

ADAB budgeted A$11,000,000 for their road construction and technical assistance programme in the hill tracts but pulled out in early 1981 and officially "decided not to renew the memorandum of understanding on the Chengi valley road project beyond its expiry date".

The roads, however, were left unfinished. The real reason for withdrawal was that Australian consultants were being attacked at work by armed hillmen.

The Australian specifications called for a 32 foot wide metalled road and the tribespeople considered it too wide for purely commercial use. Australia had been involved in similar road building projects in south and south-east Asia, particularly in hilly country known to have resistance movements. The roads in the hill tracts were being built along the Chengi valley where the Shanti Bahini, the tribal resistance movement, was most active.

Ian Gilmour, when Lord Privy Seal, confirmed in a letter to a member of the Anti-Slavery Society that "insurgents have made threats against foreign engineers engaged in road construction in the area".

UNICEF has a water supply project and WHO is seeking to eradicate malaria as part of its world-wide programme. However, tribespeople maintain that the drinking water programme benefits only military camps and Bengali families, and that the malaria eradication project was aimed at protecting army personnel only.

ADB, the main co-ordinator of the development programme in the hill tracts, reported in 1978 that it would "be prepared to consider suitable projects which fitted into the overall development approach, were meaningful on their own and preferably had a high import content". Yet the impact of 'imported' goods has been shown in many cases to be an inappropriate form of development as it affects the balance of payments, discourages the development of national industry, provides little employment and often leads to the corruption of importing agents and administrators.

If forecasts are met, 1984 will see the first oil flowing in the Chittagong Hill Tracts. That is when Bangladesh Shell Petroleum, which has made seismic surveys in the area, expects to start production. This find, though welcome to Dhaka, will mean yet more exploitation of a natural resource that will bring no benefit to the indigenous people – unless, that is, the discovery of oil creates a precedent. Shell plans to spend US$ 120 million which would be more than the total spent on all development projects in the hill tracts during the last 20 years.

According to the *Far Eastern Economic Review* of 25 August 1983, Bangladesh has suffered severely from the world-wide energy crisis. In 1973, shortly after the break-up of Pakistan, its imported oil bill amounted to only 7 per cent of its total export earnings; by 1983 it was 84 per cent. Tribal voices will not be heard in the din created by Petrobangla, the state-owned exploration and development agency, in its rush to find oil. The situation is made more alarming for the hillpeople by the injection of foreign capital in the shape of loans from Saudi Arabia ($9.2 million) and the World Bank ($23 million) for the express purpose of oil exploration. On past records, there is little hope that the Saudis will listen to the tribespeople in preference to their co-religionists in Dhaka, or that the World Bank will downgrade its purely commercial objectives.

The Joint Farming Scheme
In 1964, the Chittagong Hill Tracts Development Board set up a scheme for resettling shifting cultivators on permanent agricultural plots. This scheme, the *joutha khamar,* was intended to end *jhuming* in order to allow unhindered and accelerated exploitation of the forest and its resources.

For the Asian Development Bank the single most important task of development programmes in the Chittagong Hill Tracts is the conversion of shifting cultivators to a settled form of land usage. By 1982, the *joutha khamar* had accounted for 60 per cent of the development board's expenditure.

It is curious that the ADB should have recommended the formation of *joutha khamars* which, in essence, are collective farms. Perhaps it is not so curious that the hillpeople relocated by force on these farms were drawn from different tribes – a classic divide and rule ploy which further weakened resistance to the Dhaka authorities. It is policy for the families – and there may be as many as 60 – to be taken from different ethnic groups.

By 1982 only 24 collective farms had been established by the development board at an average cost of 0.93 million takas – about £25,000 each farm. The farms consist of poor quality agricultural land, mostly on steep slopes. The staple food, rice, cannot be grown in these conditions and farmers can only cultivate fruit trees and vegetables. Each family is allocated a plot of 5.25 acres.

Under the *joutha khamar* scheme each family has to grow an acre each of bananas, pineapples, vegetables, fruit trees and rubber plants. This requires knowledge of five different forms of production from the *jhumias* who have no experience of some of these crops. A grant to the value of 14,000 takas (£350) is provided for each family in the form of tools and fertilizers over a four year period. Inevitably, illiterate *jhumias* find it difficult to obtain grants from the development board and this difficulty is compounded by bribes which, according to tribespeople themselves, usually amount to half the total requested.

Even if the *jhumias* did receive the full grant it is unlikely that the collectives could succeed as the costings are inadequate. The total inputs per acre on *joutha khamar* rubber plantations, for example, are budgeted at only 2,115 takas (£55) over a four-year period, while the Bangladesh Forest Industries Development Corporation estimates requirements of 24,000 takas (£650) per acre.

In practice tribespeople often do not receive the full grant in one payment, unlike Bengali settlers. They may be paid on a daily basis at the rate of 20 takas per day. If they live 20 or 30 miles away, as many do, such journeys make it impossible for them to collect what is due to them.

These government rehabilitation schemes work against the interests of tribespeople and clearly favour Bengali settlers. Rarely are hillmen given 5 acre plots; usually they are allocated half or one acre per family. Many do not even manage to get their applications filled in, signed and presented to the sub-divisional officer who is locally responsible for the rehabilitation scheme. To do so often requires bribes beyond the means of the poorer hillmen. In Lama sub-division in the district of Bandarban, an area designated for rehabilitation, 2,500 Bengali and only 20 tribal families were settled in 1982.

After promulgation of martial law by General Ershad, the commissioner of Chittagong Division is no longer chairman of the board. The present chairman is *ex-officio* the GOC 24 Infantry Division and Zonal Martial Law Administrator (ZMLA) – Zone Ga (C).

Even when collective farms produce a surplus there are no marketing, storage or processing facilities controlled by the hillmen. Bengali middlemen continue to dominate marketing. The effects were described in the 1976 Asian Development Bank report:

> Every year from May until harvest time in September, the people experience an increasing shortage of victuals and the cash to produce them. They borrow money on their future harvest. One procedure is that the money-lender buys the harvest or a portion of it for one-fifth of what the crop can fetch at harvest

time (which in turn is the lowest price of the year). This practice keeps a fair proportion of the population in constant debt.

These collective farms have no recreational facilities and usually no sanitary provisions or supply of potable water, but tribespeople have little alternative to subsistence on them.

Land Dispossession

Tribespeople in the hill tracts lose their land for a variety of reasons. Sometimes this is due to their lack of understanding of its commercial value and ignorance of the concept of private property, but for the most part it is a result of trickery by Bengali entrepreneurs and government officials.

In the newly formed district of Bandarban, for example, some 80 per cent of the land is government property and is administered by the Department of Unclassified State Forest. The rest is either reserve forest or allocated to settlers. Government land is placed in three categories and valued at 40,000 takas per acre or more for class A, 15,000 – 40,000 takas for class B and 15,000 takas or less for class C.

At one village in the district, Kalaghata, government officials changed the category of land from class B to class C thereby reducing its sale price by 60 per cent. Such deceptions are common and are relatively easily perpetrated on the tribespeople.

Most are unfamiliar with the procedures for acquiring compensation for their land and are obliged to make use of Bengali middlemen. Many of these, according to the hillmen, take large commissions and even disappear entirely with the money.

As a result of both official and unofficial policies towards tribal land in the tracts the hillpeople have been unable to carry on *jhum* cultivation or use the forest in their traditional way. As a result they have become much poorer and face starvation. In desperation, some have used their land as security for loans from Bengali money-lenders. Subsequently, unable to pay the high rates of interest, they lose their land permanently.

Chapter Four
Hill Tracts for Hillmen

The indigenous peoples of the Chittagong Hill Tracts have a long history of fighting for their independence and they have always fiercely defended their territory. Even the Mughal emperors were only able to extract a tribute in cotton, the principal cash crop at the time, from the Chakmas. In 1760 the region was seceded by the Nawab Mir Qasim to the East India Company, which met the same opposition from the hillmen. In 1777, the Chakma Raja Jan Bux Khan formally declared war and after a decade of fighting signed a peace treaty in Fort William, Calcutta. Under this agreement the quasi-independent status of the hill tracts was recognised.

However, the agreement was broken as often as it was honoured. Individual traders and some farmers from the plains were allowed to enter the tracts freely, and tribespeople complained of rapes and kidnappings. The East India Company changed the system of tribute in kind, operating under the Mughals, and demanded a yearly payment in cash and, more importantly in the long run, they also recognised the chiefs of the three main tribes as revenue collectors.

In 1860, Britain officially took over the administration of the region. During most of the second half of the nineteenth century there was fighting both among the tribes and by the tribes against the British. In 1868 the British, in an attempt to bring peace to the region, set up their administrative headquarters in Rangamati in the heart of the hill tracts. The boundaries of the three major tribal territories were defined in 1884 as a further measure to check tribal warfare. What were under the East India Company fairly loosely demarcated taxation areas, became official revenue circles: the Chakma, the Mong and the Bohmong. In 1898 the British carried out a military operation which brought peace to the hill tracts but not before a joint British-Chakma expedition had finally ended the series of raids by the Kuki tribes which had plundered many Chakma villages. In that same year all the chiefs and village headmen were given many privileges, including monthly cash allowances, and an administrative system totally in the hands of local people was established. In addition, local tribal autonomy was recognised by the British. Two years later, the 1900 Regulation was promulgated which further reinforced the special status of the tracts. The many distinct tribes in the tracts historically maintained their separate cultures and it was only in the turmoil of independence that any organization managed to bring together members of different tribes.

No significant political groups appeared in the Chittagong Hill Tracts until the 1940s when the Peoples Organization was formed. It sought full autonomy and opposed incorporation into either India or Pakistan. Its slogan was "hill tracts for hillmen". Many of its members were arrested after independence in 1948 and one of its leaders, Sneh Kumar Chakma, fled to India.

For many Chakmas and other Buddhist tribespeople, the fear of religious persecution under an Islamic Pakistan led them to opt for India as Buddhism clearly has more religious and social affinities with Hinduism. For three days the flag of India flew in Rangamati during the independence turmoil.

During the 1950s and 1960s tribal students, in defiance of government regulations, organized opposition to the ban on student politics and visited hill villages where dissatisfaction was growing over the immigration of Bengalis and the dislocation caused by the Kaptai dam. In 1966, the Chittagong Hill Tracts Welfare Association was formed in an attempt to gain compensation from the government for the tribespeople, whose way of life had been ruined by the dam. The Welfare Association was disbanded during the 1971 war, having had little notice taken of its demands.

When the civil war began in 1971 many tribespeople actively supported the independence movement believing that in the new state of Bangladesh poverty would be reduced and their oppression would stop. During the war India supported the breakaway movement and many tribespeople crossed into India in order to receive military training. Many were badly treated by both the Indians and Bangladeshis and they began to fear for their future in the new country.

Towards the end of the war some of the hillmen were recruited into the Pakistani army. At the end of hostilities they were treated as collaborators. In 1972 the Bangladeshi army and Sheikh Mujibur Rahman's private paramilitary organization, the Rakki Bahini, swept into the hill tracts in search of arms and collaborators.

After the war was over weapons remained in private possession throughout Bangladesh and this included in the tracts. So as the *Far Eastern Economic Review* reported on 2 August 1980:

> The tribals say that they were left to the mercies of the Pakistani army during this period and it is strange that a tribal people dubbed as anti-Pakistani since 1947 should suddenly be seen as pro-Pakistani in 1971.

In fact, the tribespeople were not anti-Pakistani as such but fearful of the plainsmen who had always come into the tracts as exploiters. The *Review* continued:

> When the Pakistani army withdrew ... the Bangladeshi army (Mukti Bahini) came and plundered the area. Eighteen people were killed when they came out to receive the Mukti Bahini and another 16 were slaughtered in the jungle ... On December 14, 1971, 200 houses were burnt to the ground and 22 people were found sheltering in trenches in Kukichara and killed out of hand.

The Bangladeshi air force even made bombing raids on tribal villages. The immediate excuse for this operation was the unrest created by the seizure of tribal land in the Ramgarh and Bandarban sub-divisions by Bengali settlers, who had taken advantage of the chaos caused by the war to grab land.

The atrocities committed by the Bangladeshi army in the hill tracts during their 1972 reprisals led to a new political awakening of the tribespeople.

Manobendra Narayan Larma, an elected Member of the Provincial Assembly and subsequently a Member of Parliament led a tribal deputation to the Prime Minister, Sheikh Mujib, on 15 February 1972. They presented the following four demands:

1 The Chittagong Hill Tracts will be an autonomous region with its own legislature.

2 The constitution must retain the Chittagong Hill Tracts 1900 Regulation in its entirety, restoring the special status.

3 The tribal chiefs must be allowed to continue in their office with full administrative powers.

4 There must be a constitutional guarantee that the 1900 Regulation will not be amended and that Bengali families will not be allowed to settle in the area.

Mujib regarded the demand for regional autonomy as secessionist and advised the tribespeople to accept their integration into the new Bangladesh. He advised them to become Bengalis. His intransigent attitude was later to be backed by force.

Sneh Kumar Chakma, who had fled the tracts after independence and is now a leader of the Buddhist Minorities Protection Committee based in Tripura, says of this period:

> The Pakistani rulers were too far away to pay much attention to the Chittagong Hill Tracts, so whatever action they took was never intense, but with the formation of Bangladesh things changed. The problem of the tribals automatically assumed much more importance.

After the rejection of the deputation's demands, persecution was stepped up and hundreds of hillpeople fled into the more inaccessible parts of the forest and, in 1972, the Parbottya Chattagram Jana Sanghati Samity (PCJSS), the Chittagong Hill Tracts Peoples Solidarity Association, was formed.

Modern Political Consciousness
The PCJSS, which became the principal political voice of the tribespeople, was founded by two brothers, Manobendra Narayan Larma and Bodhi Priyo (alias Shantu) Larma. In 1970, after Pakistan's first elections on adult franchise, the hill tracts were allocated only one seat in the national parliament and two in the Provincial Assembly of what was then East Pakistan. Manobendra won the Provincial North seat and the Chakma chief, Raja Tridiv Roy, was elected to the National Assembly. In 1973 Manobendra was elected, on a platform of autonomy for the hill tracts, as an independent member to the first Bangladeshi Parliament. There he became a powerful spokesman for what he called "the enormity of neglect and hatred inflicted by the people from the adjoining plains to our brethren in the hills".

The PCJSS contains, besides nationalists, a number of Marxists and Maoists, but it would be wrong to assume that its structure is Marxist in character or resembles the Marxist trade unions of the plains. However, since Manobendra and Shantu Larma were Marxist followers in their student days and initially held the leading positions in the party hierarchy, the PCJSS was held to be Marxist. Moreover, when it took to direct action, its first field commander was known to employ Maoist guerrilla tactics. On the whole, it can be considered nationalistic in the sense that it strives to unite the hillpeople against the common foe, the tyrannical government in Dhaka.

The armed wing of the PCJSS is known as Gono Mukti Fouj or, more commonly, as the Shanti Bahini (Peace Force). It was formed in 1972 but became more active in 1975. According to the government it numbers only 2,000 but the Shanti Bahini itself claims 15,000. The Shanti Bahini also organizes a militia at the village level which is provided with light fire arms and acts as a local police force. Its main task is not to attack the armed forces, for which it is not adequately equipped, but to help with planting, harvesting and marketing.

Shantu Larma, who became the Shanti Bahini's field commander, was arrested in 1976. He was released in 1980, following the intervention of the Special Adviser to the President, Rajmata Benita Roy. She was later asked to resign, and although no official reason was given, it is generally accepted that her open opposition to Zia's policy in the hill tracts was the cause.

The Shanti Bahini insists that it does not receive arms from any external source. Initially, it armed itself from stocks accumulated during the independence war and since then has resupplied itself by ambushing army patrols. Although its leaders frequently cross into India to contact tribal refugees and seek international support, the Shanti Bahini maintains that it receives no finance from any foreign country or agency. However, after Sheik Mujib's assasination in 1975, its parent body, the PCJSS, is generally thought to have received tentative and short-lived support from the Indian government.

The PCJSS operates as a government in many parts of the hill tracts and has introduced its own administrative and judicial system based on the *panchayat*. This is comprised of five to 15 elected members in each village and has several levels, the lower ones electing those above. When one level fails to settle a dispute, the next is called in. The *panchayat* is also responsible for collecting taxes which it gathers, often forcibly, from non-tribespeople as well.

The PCJSS believes that the situation in the Chittagong Hill Tracts should be resolved peacefully through the political process. This was made plain in a series of letters it sent to the army GHQ Chittagong between May 1979 and May 1980, but it began to doubt the government's sincerity and ended negotiations. Dhaka remained quiet about this exchange of letters until 1981 when it dismissively said that the question of political settlement did not arise.

Major General M A Manzur, GOC Chittagong, said he would meet the Shanti Bahini leaders as the Bangladeshi government's representative. The Shanti Bahini leaders replied that since it was a political issue they preferred to talk to a civilian. However, they later agreed to have discussions with the GOC if he were formally declared to be the official representative of the government. In other words, the Shanti Bahini wanted the government to declare publicly that it recognised the Chittagong Hill Tracts issue as political and was taking the appropriate steps for a peaceful solution.

In May 1980, the tribal leaders, including the chiefs, unanimously demanded a political settlement. President Zia's response was that the

Members of the Shanti Bahini

solution lay in economic development, which clearly ruled out any possibility of a political discussion, let alone talks with the Shanti Bahini which the leaders held was absolutely essential. The negotiations with the Shanti Bahini, through Upendra Lal Chakma, were soon abandoned and the government reverted to bulldozing tactics.

In early 1980 a tribal convention was formed. The initiative for this came from the army in an attempt to counter the influence of the PCJSS and to voice apparently independent tribal criticisms of the Shanti Bahini. The general secretary of the tribal convention was Charu Bikash Chakma and one of the more powerful members was Angshue Pru Chowdhury, a government minister. The three tribal chiefs responsible for collecting taxes were also members as were various town and village leaders.

The tribal convention had no power of its own and was manipulated by Major-General Manzur. During the first few months the general secretary, at the instigation of Manzur, put forward a four point proposal purportedly to improve the situation in the hill tracts. These were:

1 Regional autonomy under which the head of administration in the districts, a chief commissioner, would be the GOC Chittagong.

2 The formation of a tribal affairs ministry which would be under the control of the chief commissioner and would act in an advisory capacity to existing government departments.

3 The formation of a special secretariat reporting directly to the president.

4 The creation of an administration responsible to a regional council of sixty representatives.

Most members of the tribal convention, including the chiefs, were under pressure from Manzur and participated out of fear of sanctions. This gave the proceedings an air of unreality since the members, although present, did not contribute. This gradually led to the disintegration of the convention which is practically defunct today.

These seemingly reasonable proposals were inherently flawed. They depended on the good will and sincerity of the chief commissioner and the president, both of whom were Bengalis. In fact, the convention had almost no support in the countryside, and its only, meagre, support in the urban areas of the hill tracts came from Rangamati and Chandraghona.

Even as a tool of government propaganda the tribal convention was a failure, although initially one or two foreign aid donors seem to have been impressed by it. For instance, the United States Agency for International Development (USAID) told Senator Cranston on 3 July 1980 that:

in an effort to reduce tensions and end the fightings, the government recently cancelled the resettlement programme, released leaders of the guerrilla movement and other tribal people from prison, and opened negotiations with tribal leaders to seek a peaceful end to the dispute. The government has taken these steps in the hope of reducing the fear of the tribal groups that they will be overwhelmed by Bengalis migrating into the hill tracts from the plains.

In contrast, representatives of SIDA, the Swedish government aid agency, met leaders of the tribal convention at Rangamati and, unconvinced by what they heard and saw, shortly afterwards withdrew their aid.

In February 1980 the government released about 100 tribal prisoners including Shantu Larma and another Shanti Bahini leader, Sabai Marma, who had been arrested four years earlier. This and the tribal convention were the two main government initiatives during 1980. But the situation had deteriorated so much that most tribespeople suspected their primary objective was to increase government credibility with aid donors.

The government refused to do anything about the most contentious issue – Bengali settlement in the district – and only a few months later began to bring in thousands of poor Bengali families.

It is not difficult to understand the distrust felt by the hillmen. Only one month after the much-trumpeted release of the prisoners, 300 tribal villagers were massacred in Kalapati by the army and Bengali settlers. The Shanti Bahini now refuses to negotiate until repression and murder stop and demands:

1 Autonomy within Bangladesh, and a separate legislature.

2 Restitution of all lands taken by Bengali immigrants since 1970 and a total ban on further immigration.

3 Constitutional arrangements for the preservation of the indigenous cultures and identities.

4 Free movement and commerce within the district.

5 Freedom from official harrassment.

Most Chittagong Hill Tracts politicians use 'autonomy' and 'self-determination' interchangeably. What is generally demanded is an autonomous province, with a separate legislature, within the framework of Bangladesh.

Border Links

Peter Niesewand in his article "Dacca sees India behind raids" in the London *Guardian* of 11 November 1981, reported raids by Shanti

Bahini fighters who had been trained in India. An estimated 500 men attacked along a 30 mile front in September and October 1981. Attacks took place in the villages of Tabalchari, Tailafangpara and Baranal on 18 September. Eight days later Matiranga village and police station came under fire and on 29 September the village of Alutila Sampara. In October the village of Khida Chari was attacked and the police station at Pachari was fired on for the second time. In these raids about 60 Bengalis died.

Niesewand said:

> ... recent attacks came when well-armed and trained Shanti Bahini crossed the Feni river frontier from India. 'There was no question of them blundering over an unmarked border in dense forest', a source here said. 'The Indian border security forces are thick on the ground on their side of the river, and it is not possible a band of 500 could have repeatedly crossed without them knowing about it'.
>
> The raids are the first large, well planned assaults on lowland Muslim settlers who have moved into the relatively unpopulated hill tracts, and have themselves frequently attacked and killed tribals, many of whom are Christian and Buddhist. In addition, the Bangladesh army has been accused of tough armed action against the tribes and in some cases of atrocities. These are impossible to check as the Bangladesh government steadfastly refuses to allow independent observers into the hill tracts.
>
> The Shanti Bahini have for years retaliated against the army by staging sporadic ambushes and occasionally engaging in pitched battles. They have also served 'quit notices' on some Muslim settlers, and have followed these up by attacks in which the new settlements have been razed.

The demands of the Shanti Bahini are similar to those of the tribespeople across the Indian border in Assam and Manipur. Large scale immigration from Nepal, Bangladesh and the Indian state of Bengal has resulted in the indigenous populations becoming a minority and losing administrative control. As a consequence there has been a succession of horrific and bloody massacres in which both settlers and tribespeople have been the victims. Law and order has broken down in India's north-eastern border states and both central and state governments seem powerless to prevent bloodshed. The army and police appear to have an ambivalent role, sometimes playing persecutor and sometimes helpless bystander. If the situation degenerates still further in the Chittagong Hill Tracts, Bangladesh may face comparable uncontrollable clashes.

The conflict between indigenous peoples and central governments is not confined just to the hill tracts and Assam. Throughout this hilly border region there are dozens of tribal, political and para-military organizations. Delhi is facing nationalist movements in the states of Meghalay, Tripura, and Mizoram as well as in Manipur and Assam. In

Burma there are as many as eight distinct nationalist movements fighting the central government.

Among those in the Bangladesh and India frontier region are the Chins, known as the Mizos in India, the Nagas and the Arakan Muslims, also called the Rohingyas.

The Calcutta journal *Frontier* on 30 August 1980 reported that:

The Rohingya (Muslim) movement drew attention when in April 1978 Burma launched Operation Naga Min to push the Rohingyas into Bangladesh after that country through its military attache in Rangoon along with Libyan assistance sought to foment a full-scale rebellion and perhaps ultimate annexation by Bangladesh of Arakan areas in Burma. It seems that at the last moment General Zia reverted to a neutral stand signalling the collapse of a Bangladeshi adventure. In fact the Rohingyas have received low-level support from across the border ever since 1948 when they expressed the desire to join their Muslim brothers as part of Pakistan.

Dhaka has fuelled the volatile situation on the Indian-Bangladeshi border by permitting freedom of movement to the Mizo National Front (MNF). After the assassination of Sheikh Mujib in August 1975, the Bangladeshi government gave shelter to the MNF. This helped to perpetuate tribal unrest in Mizoram and Tripura. The main motive was probably to foment conflict between the Mizo National Front and the Shanti Bahini and undermine the unity of the tribespeople of the hill tracts. However, the two nationalist movements have avoided conflict and the MNF do not enter Shanti Bahini territory without permission.

A union of the hillmen on all sides of the international boundaries against the plainspeople is a possibility the governments of India, Burma and Bangladesh cannot ignore. Although the problems of all the hill people differ in detail, they do face a common threat: they fear encroachment by and settlement of outsider families as well as the eventual loss of cultural identity.

The Shanti Bahini is made up almost exclusively of Chakmas, Marmas and Tripuras and it is the Tripura Youth Volunteer Army in India which is the foremost proponent of pan-tribalism.

However, there is little evidence of any formal cross-border tribal unity and even within the Chittagong Hill Tracts many of the tribespeople are suspicious that the Chakmas are seeking to restore their nineteenth century domination. As early as 1974 a small Marxist-Leninist group, the Mukti Parishad was also operating in the tracts. This is an armed wing of the Sarbohara party and is formed mainly of youths of the Tanchangya tribe. This group has not been very active since the 1970s.

The history of the hill tracts demonstrates that the tribespeople have continually struggled to preserve their independence from invaders and colonizers. Until 1947 their regional autonomy was to some extent guaranteed constitutionally but, with the creation of East Pakistan and later Bangladesh, these safeguards were whittled away. In fact, since independence, resistance by the indigenous people to the destruction of their way of life has always been met with, at best, a lack of sympathy by central government. Since the late 1970s Dhaka has responded to what is essentially legitimate political opposition with military force. This almost instinctive response has led in turn to direct action on the part of the hillmen. The result has been an escalation of fighting and the avoidable spilling of blood. Both sides have suffered, but the hillmen have suffered most.

Chapter Five
The Soil and not the People

On 25 March 1980 about 300 unarmed tribal men, women and children were massacred by Bangladeshi troops and armed Bengali immigrants at the small village of Kaokhali Bazar in Kalampati Union. The massacre was planned, according to the Member of Parliament, Upendra Lal Chakma, in retaliation against the decimation of an army patrol by tribal resistance fighters. (See Appendix 2.)

The commander of the army unit based at Kaokhali Bazar, Captain Kamal, requested tribal leaders and villagers to attend a meeting to discuss the problem of law and order and begin repair work to a Buddhist temple at Poapara. The tribal villagers gathered at 8 am. Shortly afterwards the army opened fire.

In the confusion an estimated 200 tribal people were killed and many others wounded. A mass grave containing at least 50 bodies had been dug in the confines of the local high school and more than 30 women were forcibly abducted by soldiers held for two days and repeatedly raped.

The army massacre was followed immediately by an outbreak of riots by Bengali settlers who attacked tribal families, burned down their houses and destroyed numerous Buddhist temples. At least 24 villages were affected by the violence; nine temples were attacked and five of them were completely destroyed. Entire villages were burned down and monks and nuns were among those murdered or beaten by the settlers. The home of the former Member of Parliament, Chai Thoal Roaza, was looted. The precise number of tribespeople killed and wounded during this outbreak of violence is still unknown. A detailed report sent to the Anti-Slavery Society shortly after the massacre, showed that the violence was directed particularly at priests and temples. One 60 year-old priest was robbed and had both hands broken by the Bengalis; statues and temple furniture were looted or destroyed. The report noted that the violence was aimed entirely at the tribal inhabitants and had the effect of driving many families out of the villages; not a single Bengali house was attacked during the riots.

The massacre at Kaokhali Bazar was the most serious act of violence perpetrated by the Bangladeshi army and police in the Chittagong Hill Tracts up to that time.

Militarization

British involvement in the Chittagong Hill Tracts during the raj was always minimal. Perhaps recognising the sheer physical limitations to a prolonged military campaign in the hill tracts or else having sufficient control through their alliance with the tribal chiefs, the British administration left the internal affairs of the district to its people. Under the 1900 Regulation the police force was entirely run by the tribal population as was the general administration through the tribal organization of circles and *mouzas*.

When Pakistan gained independence from Great Britain in 1947 it did not abrogate or nullify the special status of the hill tracts but ignored its contents. Bengalis settled in the area, the tribal police force was disbanded and its tribal police officers transferred to other districts of East Pakistan. Civilian tribal representatives from the tracts were also moved to other districts. The economic development carried out by the East Pakistani government, including the construction of the Kaptai dam and the Chandraghona paper mill, provided few jobs for the tribespeople and caused thousands to leave their homes.

In 1961 serious rioting took place in the hill tracts against the government programme and according to *The Statesman Weekly* of 10 May 1980, in the ensuing violence some 60,000 tribal people fled to India. The Indian government, disturbed by the influx of refugees into its sensitive north-eastern states, protested vigorously to the Pakistani government and matters improved.

It is since independence that the situation of tribespeople in the Chittagong Hill Tracts has deteriorated substantially. The first prime minister of independent Bangladesh, Sheikh Mujibur Rahman, permitted a series of reprisals to be carried out by the army and the paramilitary force of his Awami League, the Rakhi Bahini. These deepened the distrust between central government and the tribespeople. A number of hillmen were recruited by the Parkistani army during the 1971 war and this may have provoked retaliation by the victorious Bangladeshi army. However, just as many tribespeople fought with the opposing forces. In the search for the paramilitary groups created by Pakistan about 400 tribespeople were killed and hundreds of houses burned down. Protests by the hillpeople to Sheikh Mujib were met with further hostility. The new Bangladeshi government, fearing a secessionist movement, increased military activity in the hill tracts and this led to more killings.

A delegation of tribespeople led by the Member of Parliament, Manobendra Narayan Larma met Mujib and proposed that the hill tracts should become an "autonomous tribal region". This was, however, interpreted as a conspiracy against Bangladeshi sovereignty. The demand for regional autonomy, in effect the return of the conditions prevailing during the British administration, was emphatically rejected. In 1975 a second delegation, this time consisting of 67 representatives from the hill tracts met President A S Sayem and repeated their demands. Once again these were answered by renewed military violence.

The fear of secession was clearly an important factor in the recently created Bangladesh, and the need to integrate the various ethnic identities paramount. Nevertheless, the overpopulation of the rest of Bangladesh, the serious post-independence economic problems, including the prospect of famine, could not be ignored by the Father of Bangladesh, Sheikh Mujib. The resources available for exploitation in the hill tracts seemed to become one answer to these problems.

The repression of the tribespeople after 1972 was even more severe than that experienced under Pakistan. One of the reasons was that the tribespeople were demanding greater autonomy and this caused Dhaka to regard the region as a major security problem.

Matters worsened after 1975. In August of that year Sheikh Mujib was assassinated and by November the Army Chief of Staff, General Ziaur Rahman was in power. In his book, *Bangladesh: The Unfinished Revolution,* Lawrence Lifschulz argues that the Mujib assassination presaged a build-up of military power and an expansion of the intelligence services and the accompanying increase in political repression. The militarization of Bangladesh resulting from General Zia's coup also had its impact in the hill tracts. The new government in Dhaka, reported the *Far Eastern Economic Review* on 23 May 1980, was hostile to India which in turn allegedly provided arms in November 1975 and March 1977 to the Shanti Bahini.

Since 1976, there has been a massive increase in military personnel in the district. Some 30,000 regular as well as paramilitary troops had been massed by 1980 and a naval unit had been established on the artificially-created Kaptai lake. Something in the region of one-third of all regular troops are estimated to be operating in the hill tracts. The number of police stations has more than doubled since 1976 from 12 to 28.

The British government's involvement in the Chittagong Hill Tracts is in the fields of telecommunications and, whether by design or not, in the teaching of counter-insurgency techniques.

The electronics giant, Plessey Company Limited, after an approach from the Crown Agents for Overseas Governments and Administrations, supplied and installed a telecommunications network. It has links to

Chittagong and Dhaka, which is in direct contact with all police stations in the hill tracts. The Minister for Overseas Development has parliamentary responsibility for the Crown Agents and the telecommunications project was funded entirely by the British government as part of its aid programme.

In 1977 a British military mission set up a training school for officers of the Bangladeshi army. In 1983, after speculations in the British press and a series of written parliamentary questions submitted by Labour Member of Parliament Alf Dubbs (Battersea South, London), it became known that the British military presence was maintained at the Bangladesh Military Academy, Mirpur, not far from Dhaka and that it was headed by Colonel Gibson of the SAS, the Special Armed Service.

Simon Winchester, writing in the *Sunday Times* on 27 March 1983, reported that the Colonel's men had

> offered assistance to the country's military government on several occasions ... (including) ... providing equipment for dealing with insurgents in the hills east of Chittagong.

The Special Armed Service gained great experience in countering insurgents during the anti-communist battles fought in the jungles of Malaya in the 1960s.

The questions raised by Alf Dubbs were never answered on the grounds that the Foreign Office regarded them as relating to the internal affairs of a sovereign state and therefore not legitimate grounds for inquiry.

Atrocities

The strict security measures operating in the hill tracts have affected significantly the lives of the tribespeople. The Member of Parliament, Upendra Lal Chakma, has complained that the police and military presence have led to arrests and incarceration without charges. Search and destroy missions into unarmed villages are increasing. Physical abuse and the burning of homes are becoming routine and hill people are being forcibly resettled in strategic villages in order to deny civilian support to the Shanti Bahini.

On 20 August 1978 Brian Eads wrote in the *Observer* that:

> Bangladesh security forces are waging a terror campaign against the non-Bengali tribes of the Chittagong Hill Tracts which threatens the very existence of the Buddhist minority of half a million people. Official silence makes it impossible to give exact figures, but sources in the hill tracts last week gave me precise details of killings, rapes, summary arrests and detentions without trial since the end of last year. The killings and rapes are said to run into hundreds, the arrests and detentions into thousands.

The findings of Brian Eads were confirmed two years later when the Anti-Slavery Society carried out its own on-the-spot investivations. Its report contained information about a series of military atrocities:-

Early 1977   The villages of Matiranga, Guimara, Manikchari and Lakshmichari were attacked by the armed forces; 50 people were shot dead and 23 tribal women tortured to death; most of the homes were burned to the ground.

24 December 1977   The army led raids on several villages north of Rangamati; many people were arrested and detained without trial or access to legal representation.

30 December 1977   The village of Kukichara was attacked; the homes of Shanti Lal Chakma, Nathu Chandra Chakma and Sukra Moni Chakma were burned down and 12 members of Chandra Chakma's family were killed; Lal Chakma was critically wounded and Sukra Moni Chakma suffered severe injuries.

December 1978 and January 1979   About 50 villages were subject to raids to the north of Ruma army camp; number 150 Dumdumya *mouza* consisting of 22 villages had most of its houses destroyed; on 9 January 1979 all the villages in the Subalong valley were attacked; a woman of 71, Banga Kajha Chakma, was burned alive in her home during one of these raids.

5 March 1979   Two students, Samiran Talukder and Alomoy Talukder and a farmer, Rallwa Chakma, all aged 16, were arrested in the village of Gargajyachari and hacked to pieces by troops.

2 April 1979   Captain Abul Kalam Mahmud (also responsible for the massacre at Kaokhali on 25 March 1980) led a raid on the village of Kunungopara razing it to the ground: Sindhu Kumar Chakma, Arun Kanti Chakma, Anabil Chakma and others of the same family were shot dead and their bodies burned in the presence of surviving members of the family.

9 April 1979   Seventy tribespeople were arrested by the army in Rangamati, including many civilian leaders and Kalpa Ranjan Chakma, a prominent member of the ruling Bangladesh Nationalist Party; they were only released after a long period of detention and many of them had been beaten while in custody.

23 December 1979   Venerable Ajara Bhikkhu and Venerable Bannitananda Bhikkhu were murdered by members of the Bangladeshi army at the village of Thakujyammakalak; suspecting that tribal insurgents had taken shelter in Bhaisari, they attacked the village in the early hours and unable to find members of the Shanti Bahini they beat and tortured the villagers and seven died.

On 4 November 1980, Amnesty International confirming that these violations were taking place, stated that it seemed "not unlikely that the conflict is further sharpening and military confrontation could further emerge". In the same year the Shanti Bahini claimed that between 12,000 and 15,000 people were detained illegally and most of these were picked up during operations by the armed forces.

Religious persecution is commonplace. The Bangladeshi army has set up checkposts on the way to Chitmarang, one of the holiest shrines in the hill tracts and a place of pilgrimage for Buddhists. Visitors are asked for identification and thoroughly searched. Harrassment of both men and women has been such that few tribespeople now dare to visit the temple. In one incident Muslim police reviled Buddhist monks, slaughtered a cow on their robes and sprinkled blood on a statue of the Buddha.

The massive build up of army and police in the hill tracts was inevitably met by increased action by the Shanti Bahini. Some 5,000 men, supported by many tribal villages, are said to be actively fighting according to *The Statesman Weekly* of 17 May 1980. The massacre at Kaokhali on 25 March of the same year significantly took place ten days after the attack on a company under the command of Captain Kamal. Twenty-two soldiers were killed.

After the Kaokhali massacre many Bangladeshi Members of Parliament called for a Parliamentary Committee of Enquiry and what had been a domestic affair was brought to the attention of the outside world when such internationally respected publications as the London *Observer* and the *Far Eastern Economic Review* reported the bloodshed. Three opposition members, Rashed Khan Menon, Shahjahan Siraj and Upendra Lal Chakma made a tour of the area, interviewed some 500 hillpeople and made their findings public at Dhaka's National Press Club on 25 April 1980.

Their recommendations were that a judicial inquiry into the massacre take place, that the tribal people be provided with proper security, that all Buddhist temples be restored and compensation made and that the Bengali settlers be withdrawn from the hill tracts. They concluded:

The existing problems are fully political by nature and should be solved politically.

The Members of Parliament also observed:

In the name of providing food and shelter, poor helpless people from a different district are being led against the oppressed and innocent of the Chittagong Hill Tracts. This is not only an ignoble and inhuman plan but also a conspiracy directed against the poor people of the Chittagong Hill Tracts and other districts of Bangladesh ... The sinister motive of the government is clear from the fact that the district administration attempts to express ignorance about the influx of settlers, but it is on the other hand busy with rehabilitating refugees on the hearth and home of the tribals.

In response the government promised an inquiry, released some 100 tribal prisoners and two rebel leaders, Chabai Larma and Shantu Larma. A five man parliamentary committee headed by the Home Minister, Mustafizur Rahman, was set up but none of its findings has been made public, if indeed it has ever made any. Furthermore, the committee did not include members of the opposition or Chittagong Hill Tracts representatives. The establishment of the parliamentary inquiry raised hopes for a peace initiative and Major General Manzur, GOC of the Chittagong Hill Tracts, was instructed by the Bangladeshi government to enter into a dialogue with the Shanti Bahini.

The tribal convention of 1980 (see Chapter 4) was devised in a further bid to reduce tension in the hill tracts. Charu Bikash Chakma, a member of the tribal elite, became general-secretary and proposed that the land of the hill tracts be divided in a ratio of 2:1, with two acres of land reserved for the tribespeople for every one offered to outsiders. This was unacceptable to the hillmen.

These initiatives were essentially cosmetic. In December 1980 the Home Minister, Mustafizur Rahman, the same man heading the parliamentary inquiry into the Kaokhali massacre, introduced the Disturbed Areas Bill. The bill, which became law in early 1981, gave police and the army unrestricted powers to shoot anyone suspected of anti-state activities. The lowest officer ranks were empowered to fire on anyone or make an arrest without warrant in any defined politically disturbed areas. The bill was greeted by massive opposition for it was a further step in the militarization of Bangladesh generally. Upendra Lal Chakma, stated:

> the government is looking for a genocidal solution to the problems of ethnic minorities up there.

The genocidal solution had been heralded on 26 May 1979 when Brigadier Hannan and Lieutenant-Colonel Salam, in an unguarded moment, declared at a public meeting in Panchari that "we want the soil and not the people of the Chittagong Hill Tracts".

On 28 April 1981, *The Guardian* argued that the army and police would be immune from challenge in the courts and could enter any premises without warrant. For the paramilitary opposition the Act was seen as sanctioning violations of human rights. Such legislation is indeed extraordinary since even legislation enacted in war time, such as the Defence of India Rules passed during the Second World War or the Defence of Pakistan Rules promulgated during 1965 do not provide such powers of shooting to kill as are provided under the proposed Disturbed Areas Act.

The International Commission of Jurists' *Review,* No 30, July 1983, pointed out that Bangladesh's

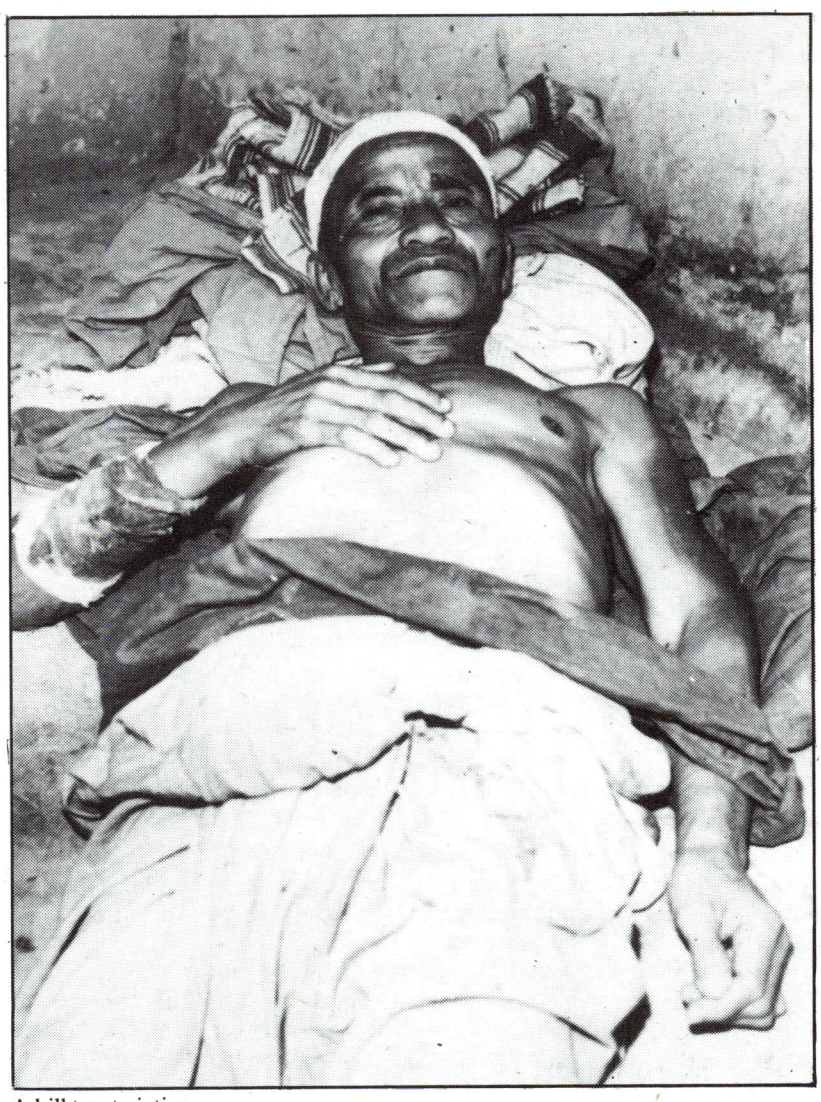

A hill tract victim

Martial Law Tribunals and Courts have the power to try any offence punishable under the martial law regulations and orders or any other law. The proceedings under the tribunal are held *in camera*. The chairman of the tribunal may require any person participating in the proceedings to take an oath of secrecy not to disclose anything that has come to his knowledge in, or in connection with the trial. The procedure before the tribunal and the martial law courts is one of summary trial. There are also changes in the customary rules as to the burden of proof. The accused cannot be defended by a lawyer, but may be helped and advised by a person approved by himself ('a friend of the accused'). The martial law courts provide for trial of an accused person *in absentia*. There is no right of appeal and no court including the Supreme Court can question any order, verdict, sentence or trial procedure of martial law courts.

One year after Upendra Lal Chakma made public the details of the Kaokhali massacre, he was once more protesting against military and police abuses. At a press conference in Dhaka on 1 April 1981 he said: "The rate and intensity of unabated repression have increased so much that no conscientious citizen can remain safe any more".

He recounted incidents of human rights violations that took place in the Chittagong Hill Tracts between September 1980 and March 1981. He appealed to fellow politicians "to take the necessary steps to stop the unabated looting, killing, arson, rape and eviction of the tribals from their land, dishonour of religious feelings and sentiment".

Only two months later, on 26, 27 and 28 June 1981, government-backed riots took place in the Matiranga Police Station area and about 500 tribal men, women and children died. Many were hacked to death, some burned alive and whole villages were razed to the ground. The armed forces had previously confiscated guns held by the tribal people in the area and during the rioting had made no attempt to restore order. Once more, Upendra Lal Chakma called at another press conference on 9 July 1981 for a parliamentary committee of inquiry to investigate these crimes. Again his pleas were ignored (see Appendix 3).

The following eyewitness account of military brutality, originally written in Bengali, and dated 20 August 1983, was sent to the Chakma Rajguru, The Venerable Aggavansa Mahathero.

On 26 June 1983 the Bangladeshi armed forces started a bombing operation in the area of Panchari Police Station and entered the neighbouring villages. The young men fled for fear of death. During the nights of 26 and 27 July they arrested, among others, Mr Birendra Kumar Chakma (65) a Union Council Member; Mr Jyotirmoy Dewan (33), headmaster of Taraban Primary School, and his colleague, Mr Lalan Bihari Chakma (27). Hot water was poured into the eyes of Mr Dewan. The whereabouts of Mr Lalan Bihari Chakma and the others are still unknown.

On 11 July, 12 members of two families in the village of Golakpatimachara were shot dead. Among them were three women and five children under six.

On the night of 9 August, 10 people including Mr Juddha Chandra Chakma (55), headmaster of Tarabanchara Primary School were picked up and are still missing. On 10 August, 100 houses in the Maramaichyachara village were burned to ashes and 120 houses in Jedarmaichyachara village were set on fire on the same day. Ten people arrested at the time are still missing.

On 11 August, 150 houses in the village of Logang were burned down and some innocent people taken away. Their whereabouts could not be traced. The Bangladeshi army entered the village of Tarabanya on the same day and indescribably oppressed the innocent villagers. Muslim settlers, accompanying the army, hacked 50 people, including Mr Surendra Tripura (40) and his wife (67), to death, and looted the villagers. They lifted two or three four- and five-year-olds up bodily by their limbs and smashed them to the ground. The Venerable Bodhipal Bhikkhu, Head Monk of the Banavihar Buddhist Temple in the village of Jedamaichyachara, was beaten the same day and he left for Agartala, Tripura, India as he could not bear the military oppression any more.

The government-countenanced violence dating back to the 1960s and the massacres following the 1972 war and that at Kaokhali in 1980 induced terror in tribal villagers. They abandoned their homes and fled to the safety of the forest. Some have remained there while others have escaped across the border into India. According to the 16 January 1980 statement of the PCJSS 60,000 tribespeople fled into India after the 1961 riots. More fled in the aftermath of the 1971 war and, in 1977, 5,000 crossed into Tripura. In 1978, about 25,000 Chakmas entered Mizoram after more than 50 of their villages were attacked. In 1981, after the bloodletting at Kaokhali and Matiranga, about 15,000 abandoned the hill tracts.

Many of these refugees have remained in the neighbouring Indian state of Tripura where, in 1981, there were 14 refugee camps. Every visitor to the refugees was met with a constant refrain: "If we had not left, we would have been killed by the Muslims", reported the Calcutta newspaper, *Sunday* on 25 October 1981. *The Times of India,* on 5 October 1981, estimated that there were some 40,000 refugees from the tracts living in various Indian border states.

The burgeoning refugee problem was briefly alleviated in October 1981 when the Indian and Bangladeshi governments came to an agreement over the return of the tribespeople. Some went back during early 1982 but little is known of their fate. Many are supposed to have been resettled on the *joutha khamars,* the co-operative farming estates. Others, after receiving assurance of rehabilitation on their own land, were simply given 150 takas (about £4).

Many refugees found their houses and other properties and possessions in Bengali hands. Destitute, they fled to other areas and some took shelter with relatives. Some tried to survive on yams and other wild fruits and roots and a great number died of starvation.

The threat to life is accompanied by other forms of human rights violations perpetrated by the armed forces in the full knowledge of the Bangladeshi government. The Anti-Slavery Society has received detailed allegations of ill-treatment of Buddhist tribesmen and other people held in army custody. Beatings of detainees are common and boys are crippled to prevent their carrying arms. Forced confessions are extracted by electric shocks, by the witholding of food and water, by half drowning and by other forms of ill-treatment. Some prisoners are held in underground pits where they remain for weeks. Young girls and women are regularly raped by police and army personnel. This is done both as a form of torture and in an attempt at genocide. Unmarried mothers are unacceptable to tribal communities and they have no alternative but to leave the tracts. They frequently become Muslims and Dhaka encourages Bengali men to marry tribal women.

The tribespeople of the hill tracts face increasing military violence and attrition. On 29 July 1983, *The Times of India* reported that there had been 95 deaths from malaria in "different remote tribal villages ... during the past 20 days." Although malaria is endemic in the region, such high death rates suggest deteriorating living conditions and medical support services.

Checkpoints set up by the armed forces in some areas have disrupted internal trading. This has resulted in a shortage of food and other necessities for families living in remote parts of the tracts. Tribespeople carrying such daily essentials as grain and kerosene are often harrassed and frequently their goods are confiscated; even medicines and medical prescriptions are seized. Army personnel dressed as civilians often patrol markets to make arbitrary arrests and now tribespeople are increasingly staying away from towns and villages.

But by the summer of 1981 even some factions in the army wanted a political settlement. Unfortunately, they were unable to carry Zia with them. Peter Niesewand reported in *The Guardian* on 29 July 1981 that a confidant of Zia's had told him:

> We are doing some wrong there. We are being unfair to the tribes. It is a political problem that is being dealt with by police and army action, yet it can be settled politically very easily. We have no basis for taking over these lands and pushing the tribes into a corner. We should at least call a meeting of these tribal leaders and ask them their demands.

These actions have amounted to an economic blockade which has forced up prices. In 1983 rice sold at up to 200 per cent of its market price; paraffin and salt are scarce. The continuing militarization and the restrictions placed on the movement of essential supplies must be seen as a direct attack on the lives of the tribespeople.

Perhaps a clue to the perceptions of Dhaka is inadvertently contained in a press release issued in London by the High Commissioner for Bangladesh and which was sent to the Anti-Slavery Society on 2 February 1981. It was in response to the Society's criticism of government policy in the hill tracts, criticism considered by the High Commission as appearing "to be designed to malign Bangladesh". The release said that

> The present Government of Bangladesh is devoted to building up the country on the basis of Bangladesh nationalism. For the purpose of achieving a balanced development of all areas of the country, the Government has given special attention to the backward and tribal population for whom special facilities exist.

Those special facilities were not enlarged upon.

Chapter Six
Just Time to Stop Genocide

On 3 October 1983 the Chief Martial Law Administrator, General Ershad, declared a pardon for what he called "the misguided elements in the Chittagong Hill Tracts". Addressing meetings in Khagrachari, Bandarban and Rangamati, he announced a six point rehabilitation programme for members of the Shanti Bahini who surrendered before 25 February 1984; this was later extended to 26 April 1984. The offer included £250 in cash, grain, five acres of land, jobs in the security forces, vocational training abroad and elegibility for local elections. "Those who come out of their hideouts and surrender to the authorities have nothing to be afraid of since the government has come forward with a liberal attitude of forgiveness," he stated.

He went on to promise a new hill tracts manual that would suit the needs of the tribal people and preserve their interests. Furthermore, a special five year development plan was to be implemented which would designate the Chittagong Hill Tracts a "special economic zone". Measures to set up more industries, develop agriculture and co-operatives as well as provide increased educational and job opportunities were announced.

It will be difficult for the tribespeople to take these promises seriously. Other development initiatives, from the Kaptai dam to the Chittagong Hill Tracts Development Board, have provided few benefits and caused widespread landlessness and greater poverty. The measures do not answer the main criticisms levelled by the Shanti Bahini against the government. They do not halt the settlement programme that has caused so much conflict in the last decades nor do they reduce the military presence in the hill tracts.

By February 1984, fewer than 100 of the estimated 3,500 active members of the Shanti Bahini had surrendered to the authorities. Furthermore, it has been reported to the Anti-Slavery Society that even those who have given themselves up have not received the money and land promised by Ershad.

The activities of the Shanti Bahini have not diminished. They continue to receive assistance from inside India and of all the numerous guerrilla forces operating in the Bangladesh, India and Burma border region, they are perhaps the best trained and equipped. On 19 January 1984 it was reported that three foreigners working for Shell, which is prospecting for oil in the hill tracts, were kidnapped by the Shanti Bahini. The employees, a New Zealander, a Dutchman and an American were held for ransoms reported to be as high as £200,000. The company has so far refused to make public the details, but it is understood that the bulk of the ransom was paid in Indian rupees, a currency difficult to obtain in Bangladesh.

But if the resistance is not dead, neither are the offensives of the Bangladeshi army. All aspects of life in the hill tracts continue to be affected by the armed forces. Areas are given security ratings and categorised into green (friendly), white (neutral) and red (hostile). In the red zones the Bangladeshi army is facing persistent resistance from the Shanti Bahini and nobody can enter without the prior permission of the military authorities. The army and paramilitary forces are able to behave much as they like in these localities, acquiring vast areas as camps and helping Bengalis establish settlements. Recent visitors to the hill tracts have stated to the Anti-Slavery Society that "soldiers are everywhere and road blocks are set up at regular intervals on all roads. Identification papers are required throughout the hill tracts".

Bangladeshi journalists who have reported on the conflicts have faced harrassment and persecution. Saleem Samad, a journalist with the Dhaka newspaper, *New Nation,* was recently detained for several days without food and water. Another journalist investigating conditions in the hill tracts, Sunil Kanti De, was arrested in June 1981 and continues to languish in prison. Amnesty International reported that he had been tortured and was unable to walk.

Sadly, persecution of tribespeople and their sympathisers has not abated. Far from the situation improving since Ershad seized power conditions for the peoples of the tracts have worsened. The peace offer of October 1983 is seen by tribespeople as little more than an elaborate propaganda exercise timed to coincide with a series of foreign tours: Bangladesh was visited shortly afterwards by the Queen and Canadian Prime Minister Pierre Trudeau.

The prospects for the predominantly Buddhist tribal population of the Chittagong Hill Tracts are not hopeful. Elsewhere in Bangladesh smaller and less isolated communities of tribal minorities such as the Garos, the Santals and the Paharis, have faced similar discrimination and persecution in the past; today they are weakened, landless and marginalised. The Chittagong Hill Tracts continue to be the homeland for people with a way of life different from the majority in Bangladesh. The future of these people, as this report shows, is in jeopardy. The policies of militarization and internal colonization taken to their logical conclusions can only end in further loss of life and the destruction of a distinctive culture.

It is the view of the Anti-Slavery Society that urgent action is needed now if genocide is to be forestalled. The Bangladeshi people have themselves struggled for their independence from British and subsequently Pakistani rule; they will undoubtedly understand why tribespeople in the hill tracts aspire to greater self-determination. To deny these aspirations is to deny them rights recognised under international law.

In particular the United Nations International Covenant on Civil and Political Liberties, Article 1 declares:

> All peoples have the right to self-determination. By virtue of that right they freely determine their political status and freely pursue their economic, social and cultural development ...

and Article 27 declares:

> In those states in which ethnic, religious or linguistic minorities exist, persons belonging to such minorities shall not be denied the right, in community with the other members of their group, to enjoy their own culture, to profess and practise their own religion, or to use their own language.

In the United Nations International Convention on the Elimination of all Forms of Racial Discrimination, Article 5 declares that:

> In compliance with the fundamental obligations laid down in Article 2 of this Convention, States Parties undertake to prohibit and to eliminate racial discrimination in all its forms and to guarantee the right to everyone, without distinction as to race, colour, or national or ethnic origin, to equality before the law ...

In the International Labour Organisation's Convention 107, concerning the protection and integration of indigenous and other tribal and semi-tribal populations in independent countries, Article 11 declares:

> the right of ownership, collective or individual, of the members of the populations concerned over the lands which these populations traditionally occupy shall be recognised.

Furthermore, in the joint statement submitted to the United Nations Working Group on Indigenous Populations in its inaugural session in August 1982 and supported by the indigenous delegates it was stated that:

> Indigenous peoples and groups shall be entitled freely and independently to practise, develop, and perpetuate their own religions, languages, cultures, traditions, social systems and ways of life.

A new policy from the Bangladeshi government aimed at providing tribal autonomy and guaranteeing rights is a necessity. The Anti-Slavery Society recommends most earnestly that the Government of Bangladesh:

1   enter into discussions with all sectors of tribal society in the Chittagong Hill Tracts with a view to reaching a political settlement which would respect the land rights, future and identity of the indigenous peoples;

2   bring an immediate halt to the influx of settlers into the tracts;

3   reduce the number of troops operating in the tracts;

4   investigate human rights violations against tribal peoples in the hill tracts.

The Society further recommends to international funding agencies and national governments providing development aid for projects in the Chittagong Hill Tracts that they withdraw support where such projects are against the wishes and interests of the indigenous population and that all future projects are carried out only after consultation with indigenous peoples' representatives.

Finally, the Anti-Slavery Society urges the Government of Bangladesh to allow free access to the troubled region to international observers and journalists. This measure alone would do much to reduce the level of fear and suspicion of the people of the hill tracts.

Appendices

SECRET

Commissioner
Chittagong Division

Memo No. 665-C

To: Mr.

It has been decided that landless/river erosion affected people from your district will be settled in Chittagong Hill Tracts (CHTs). The settlement will be done in selected Zones and each family will be given Khas land free of cost according to the following scale:-

Plain land	$2\frac{1}{2}$ acres.
Plain and bumpy mixed	4 acres
Hilly land	5 acres

It has been decided that you will send 5,000 families.

You are requested to collect particulars of intending and suitable families from the Chairman of the concerned Union Parishads sought them out and furnish list to the Deputy Commissioner, CHTs through special messenger by the 30th of Sept./80 at the latest. To keep paper record of the selected settlers, group leaders and issue of Identity card in all the districts in an uniform manner, detail guidelines have been prepared (copy enclosed) so that you can ensure strict compliance of the concerned Union Parishad Chairman.

It is the desire of the Govt. that the concerned Deputy Commissioner will give top priority to this work and make the programme a success.

You are requested to immediately call a meeting of the concerned Chairman, Union Parishads and give them detailed instructions in the matter.

I would like to have a report about the action taken by you in the matter by 15.9.80 positively for information of the Govt.

Sd/Saifuddin Ahamed,
5-9-80
Commissioner
Chittagong Division

SECRET

Govt. of the Peoples Republic of Bangladesh,
Office of the Deputy Commissioner, CHTs.

Memo No. 1025 (9) C   Dt. Rangamati, 15th Sept./80

From: Mr. Ali Haider Khan,
         Deputy Commissioner,
         Chittagong Hill Tracts.

To: Mr. ....

Sub: Settlement of landless non-tribal families in CHTs.-2nd Phase

With reference to our discussion in Dacca on 21-8-80 and reference to Commissioner, Chittagong Division's letter No. 66(9)/C dt. 4-9-80 on the above noted subject, I furnish below a guideline regarding the programme of settlement of landless non-tribal families from other districts in CHTs:-

1) Selection of families should be completed by 15th Oct. 80
2) The Chairman of the Union Parishads concerned will issue identity cards to the selected families in the forma enclosed at Annexene (A)
3) Names of families groupwise should be sent to us by 22nd October/80. On receipt of these lists we shall decide as to where they will be rehabilitated and shall indicate to you on which dates the groups should report to the reception centre at the Haji camp (pilgrimage camp), Chittagong.
4) At the reception centre an officer will take care of the settlers and will make arrangements for their journies to the rehabilitation blocks. The settlers will however, arrange their own food.
5) At the reception centre settlers will be given taka 200/- per family and on their arrival at their rehabilitation blocks they will be paid another instalment of taka 500/-. After that, each family will be given further grants (C) taka – 200/- per month for five more months. In addition for 6 months the settlers will be given 12 seers of wheats per family per

week under Food For Work Programme for construction of their own houses, reclaiming their lands, making village roads for them and for digging tanks in their own paras (areas). For another six months there will be provision for wheat under strict Food For Work Programme.

6) In rehabilitation blocks each family will be settled with Khas land at the following rate:
   1) 5 acre hilly land
   2) 4 acres mixed land
   3) 2.5 acres paddy land

I enclose here with an annexure 'B' an instruction for the Chairman of the Union Parishad where from the families will be sected.

Sd/ Ali Haider Khan
D.C.
Chittagong Hill Tracts

*A statement by Mr Upendra Lal Chakma, Member of Parliament,
Bangladesh, at his Press Conference held at the Assembly Hall, Dhaka on
1 April 1980*

KAOKHALI MASSACRE: BANGLADESH ARMY SLAUGHTERS CIVILIANS IN CHITTAGONG HILL TRACTS.

In the morning of 25 March 1980, an estimated 300 tribal civilian men, women and children were massacred by regular Bangladesh Army troops (operating in conjunction with armed Bengali immigrants) at Kaokhali Bazar, Kalampati Union, Betbunia Thana, Chittagong Hill Tracts. Available evidence suggests that the massacre was planned, possibly linked in retaliation against the decimation of an army patrol by resistance tribal fighters (Shanti Bahini) in early March in Subolong area, Barkal Thana, Chittagong Hill Tracts.

Since the independence of Bangladesh in 1971, conflict within the Chittagong Hill Tracts has escalated. The root of the problem has been the imposition of Bangladesh immigrants, culture and laws into a tribal, resource-rich area, which under Pakistan (and formerly British)law had been treated as a special "excluded area" where local laws, autonomy, and restrictions against Bengali immigration from the over-populated plains districts (Noakhali, Comilla, and Chittagong) had been in force. Tensions increased to a point where local tribal armed resistance developed, through a resistance group called the Shanti Bahini – a guerilla force estimated at about 15,000 tribal youths. Progressively, the Bangladesh Government response has been military subjugation. Over the past four years, regular army troops – now numbering 6-8 brigades of 1 Division – has undertaken the following repressive measures in an effort to control the resistance: (1) arrest and incarceration of tribals without charges or recourse to legal protection; (2) search-and-destroy missions into unarmed villages, including physical abuse and burning of homes and fields; (3) establishment of "ideal villages" of resettled (forcibly) tribals in an effort to deny the resistance a civilian base of support; (4) massive Government-sponsored migration (including financial incentives) of Bengalis from overpopulated plains districts into tribal areas; (5) introduction of supposedly development projects in order to exploit natural resources and to facilitate troop movement and combat effectiveness (new roads, cantonments, etc) and (6) formation of "tribal convention", supposed tribal leaders without broad-based support, who provides civilian legitimacy to army actions.

Armed conflict between army and resistance fighters has escalated recently, often with innocent civilians being used as pawns or scapegoats by the army. In early March, a 22-member army patrol led by Major Mosin Reza in the midst of a search-and-destroy mission in the Subolong Bazar area, Barkal Thana, CHT, was ambushed by the Shanti Bahini. All soldiers were killed. Possibly in retaliation, a Captain Kamal of Kaokhali Bazar Army Camp requested tribal leaders and villagers to attend a meeting at the Bazar to discuss the law and order problem and to plan reconstruction work of several Buddhist temples, at 8 am on 25 March 1980. At 9 am of the same day rifle fire suddenly broke out. The events during the confusion can not be reconstructed definitely. However, by the end of the shooting spree – exacerbated by armed Bengali civilians joining in the military attack – an estimated 200 tribal men, women and children had been brutally murdered. The Bazaar incident then spread with several Buddhist temples attacked, monks and nuns were mercilessly killed or wounded, and about two dozen villages in the union were attacked, some burned to the ground. The exact human toll is unknown but certainly exceeds 200. Massive migration of the affected tribal communities has taken place. Lists of the villages affected, temples destroyed, known individuals killed or wounded are appended to this document.

Although no official army report has been made public to account for the massacre, one informal explanation offered has been that resistance fighters initiated the firings. This explanation seems highly implausible, for several reasons: (1) the army itself called the preplanned meeting; (2) armed Bengali civilians who joined in the killing appeared prepared to participate; (3) no casualties were reported from either the army or the Bengali marauders; (4) the army has refused an impartial investigation; (5) Government has attempted to suppress the massacre news; and (6) public demands by the member of Parliament representing the CHT for a full investigation reported in the Bengali newspapers have been totally ignored.

ACTIONS INDICATED
1 The massacre should be given wide scale publicity to ensure that Government and the military recognize the need for accountability and to reduce the likelihood of a recurrence.
2 Governments committed to human rights and non-governmental groups committed to protecting the rights of minorities and civilians against armed military attacks should demand Bangladeshi Government accountability, full investigation, preferably by an impartial commission – either impartial Bangladeshi or international in character.
3 Governments and agencies with active "development assistance

programmes in the CHT – including Australia and the UNDP/Asian Development Bank – should immediately cease development projects in the CHT. These projects have excluded tribals from the employment generated, have created physical facilities and infrastructures that have either assisted the army's counter-insurgency actions or facilitated immigration of Bengalis into tribal lands. Sweden, which formerly supported a forestry project in the CHT, has completely withdrawn its assistance activities in the CHT.

4 The Bangladesh Government and army should immediately desist from the anti-human rights tactics of imposing a military solution on a problem of ethnic, cultural and economic conflict.

5 Negotiation should be initiated to explore for a political solution to the CHT problem. A solution should recognize the legitimate concerns of the tribals against ethnic, cultural, economic and social annihilation by the Government's policies and massive immigration.

ANNEXURE

Tribals killed at Kaokhali	*Buddhist Temple Affected*
Kumud Bikash Talukdar (Bazaar Chowdhury)	Betchari*
Shashi Dev Chakma (Chairman, Paopara H.S.)	Headmanpara
Aswini Kumar Karbari	Kashkhalimukhpara
Aswini Kumar Chakma	Tanghapara*
Kalimohan Karbari (Postmaster)	Rangeypara
Udayan Kumar Chakma (Headmaster, Bara, Dalu)	Puapara
Dinanath Chakma (Director, Co-op Society)	Chote Dalu*
Bijoy Kumar Chakma	Bara Dalu*
La Theai Marma (Ex-Member, Union Council)	Tripuradighi*
Kalanjoy Chakma (Ex-Freedom fighter)	
Krishna Hari Chakma (Ex-Malaria Supervisor)	*Temple completely destroyed

Tribals taken to hospital
Parimal Kanti Chakma – Rangamati Sadar Hosp.   25-28 March (by Army per)
Indus Kumar Chakma   ”   ”   ”   25 March (admitted by army pei
Ittukya Chakma – Chittagong Medical Hosp.

Eye-Witness to Massacre
Sai Theai Karbari, ex-Chairman, Kalampati Mouza

Kaokhali Villages Affected:
24 villages – largest and most affected including: Kachukhalimukh (80 families); Betchari (80 families); Rangeypara (70 families); Chote Dalu (80 families); Bara Dalu (80 families).

Appendix 3
Press Statement by Upendra Lal Chakma, July 1981

Venue
Central Office,
Jatiyo Samajtantrik Dal

Date
09 July, 1981.
Time
17-00 Hours

Gentlemen from the Press,

I am drawing your kind attention with a heavy heart to a most barbaric incident in the Hill Tracts. I hope, for the greater interest of the nation, you will give due coverage of the incident in your respective newspapers.

The 11-square-mile-area of Gomti-Belchari Union of Matiranga Police Station under Ramgarh sub-division of Chittagong Hill Tracts, inhabited mainly by the tribals, has been ravaged by a savage government-backed riot on the 26th, 27th and 28th June, 1981. Thousands of new settlers continued their acts of arson and atrocities for three days under the aegis of different law-enforcing agencies in the whole area. Hundreds of the tribals were looted and burnt to ashes. About 500 tribals, young and old, men, women and children, were mercilessly slaughtered with sharp-edged weapons. Some of them were burnt alive. We have got some of the names of the victims. The worst affected areas were Katun Karbari Village of 187 Gargaria Nal Mouza, Jogondra Huadnan Village, Dhanuchara Village, Brajon Kumar Village, Manik Village and Kinadhan Village of 183 Khodachara Mouza. Thousands of people, presumed to be killed, are still missing.

Government forces instigated the riot which devastated the whole area of Gargaria Nal, Gomti, Badalchara, Changrakaba, Bolchari, Ajodhya, Khedachara, Alutila, Dhallya, Toikadong, Daldali, Matiranga and Ojachu Mouza covering three thousand tribal families who became destitute and homeless over-night. Many of them crossed the border to save their lives and took refuge in India. Others took shelter in the deep forest ignoring the monsoon.

Before this incident, Government forces tactfully seized the licensed fire-arms of the tribals in order to facilitate the rioters. They took away the fire-arms of Anna Kumar Tripura of Alutila Headman Village and Mr Bali Mogh, Mongla Mogh and Ganga Mohan Tripura of Khedachara

Mouza. New settlers looted and burnt the houses of the tribals in broad day light before the eyes of the Police and Army personnel who took no initiative to quell the rioters. Not only that, Mr. Kamini Kumar Tripura, an ex-Member of Belchari Union and his neighbours were refused shelter when they approached the Army Camp, at Matiranga on the 27th June, the second day of the holocaust.

I vehemently condemn this inhuman and ignoble massacre, acts of killing and arson and, at the same time, strongly demand to form an impartial Enquiry Commission with an Honourable Judge from the High Court and Members both from the Treasury and Opposion bench. I also demand for the explanatory punishment of the culprits and adequate compensation for the affected families. Proper arrangement should also be made for the safe return of those who had to take shelter in India for the security of their lives.

Thanks to you all.

Sd./- Illegible. 09-07-81.
(Upendra Lal Chakma)
Member of Parliament

Appendix 4
Particulars of Reserve Forests in the Chittagong Hill Tracts

1 **Area of the forests before the closure of**
   Kaptai dam:
   Chittagong Hill Tracts (Northern Part) = 679.5 square miles
   Chittagong Hill Tracts (Southern Part) = 321.99 square miles
   Unclassified State Forests = 3,400.00 square miles

2 **Area of forests after closure of the dam:**
   Chittagong Hill Tracts (Northern Part) = 617.00 square miles
   Chittagong Hill Tracts (Southern Part) = 315.00 square miles
   Unclassified State Forests = 3,166.00 square miles

3 **Area of forests dereserved and occupied**
   by the Kaptai project:
   Chittagong Hill Tracts (Northern Part) = 44.50 square miles
   Chittagong Hill Tracts (Southern Part) = 2.25 square miles
   Plantations = 2.25 square miles

4 **Area of Sangu Reserve Forest** = 128.25 square miles

5 **Area of Matamuhuri Reserve Forest** = 160.71 square miles

A Memorandum submitted by the tribal people of the CHT before the Deputy Chief Martial Law Administrator, Major General Ziaur Rahman, who had come as head of the Fact-Finding Committee to Rangamati (in January 1976)

Your Honour,

Due to geographical conditions and the customs of the people, and also the constitutional history of CHT, the problems of this part of the nation are different from those of the other parts of the land.

The construction of the Kaptai dam and the resulting problems have made the situation more complicated. Under the colonial regime, no attempt was made to understand the problems of this part of the nation. In the field of development, it has always been neglected. It is a fact that after independence, we were given much hope from the side of the Government, but in reality, there was no basis for such hope (i.e., mere words).

On February 15, 1972, the tribal chief and other leaders signed and submitted a memorandum which embodied the hopes and aspirations of their people, who up until that time had been completely neglected. Later, other tribal leaders submitted similar memoranda which met with the same fate.

It is very encouraging to us that the present Government is casting its eyes with kindness toward this ever-neglected people. Because of this new outlook and goodwill, we now have this opportunity to present to you the following proposals:

To the President:

Among the inhabitants of the CHT, those who come from the tribal community are the real and original sons of the soil. They therefore claim that they should receive first consideration in any of the programmes initiated in this area.

At the time of partition in the year 1947, the percentage of hill people was 97 per cent. In subsequent years, without the migration of infiltrators and the floating population from outside the country, the proportion of the original population of the country would have remained the same. It has not. Under such circumstances, if any programme is to be realistic, all development schemes should keep the interests of the tribal people in mind. Otherwise, any such programme is bound to be fruitless.

The only hydro-electric project of the nation is located in this district.

It is a matter of pride for the people here. The vast expanse of water captured by the dam provides a scene that impresses every visitor with its beauty. But could anybody have thought that this immense body of water is to some extent filled with the tears of the local people? Through the cables of the electric lines not only current flows, but also the sighs of grief. For the general benefit of this country, no other project alone, we can claim that we have fulfilled our responsibility for another fifty years. Hence, our appeal to our honourable President is that in the formulation of future development programmes, attention will be given to the development of the people who have suffered so that in the name of development, it does not open the door to exploitation by the infiltrators.

Oh Honourable President,

May the above appeal of these neglected people of this area be accepted with kindness. With this hope, we are submitting the following recommendations for your approval and immediate implementation:

The educational backwardness of these tribal people is proverbial. Toward educational upliftment, we ask that:

a) grants to non-government institutions be increased;

b) one government college be set up in each of the divisions of Khagrachari and Bandarban. The Government should at least give affiliation and monetary grants to the two newly erected colleges at Khagrachari and Bandarban;

c) in all educational institutions, an adequate reservation of seats for tribal students should be made;

d) for the tribes who have not yet been attracted by education, the Government should take adequate measures to provide stipends for their education;

e) the amount of the stipends for the Buddhist students should be increased;

f) provision should be made for stipends for the Tipras and other tribes;

g) in the field of higher education, provision should be made for special local and foreign scholarships;

h) the present system of distributing scholarships should be changed and instead a committee should be formed with both Government and non-government members.

One of the main steps toward economic upliftment of our country or nation is business (production and trade). For many years, this role has been monopolized by the plains people in such a way that there is no chance for the tribal people to enter this field. For the overall development of the tribal people, we need the following facilities: Some plots in shopping centres should be kept reserved for tribal people; arrangements should be made for easy term industrial and commercial loans; a tax holiday for new businesses and the opportunity to obtain licences and permits, so that they need not face hard competition from the plains people.

From time immemorial, the hill people have lived on *jhum* cultivation as their main source of income, but the fertility of the *jhum* land has decreased. Cultivation using this system has had to be abandoned, and in the absence of any other resources, the economic condition of the people has deteriorated. The most fertile portion of the cultivable land, has been drowned. This has made the contemporary problem more acute. In this connection, it may be mentioned here that the Government has completely failed to rehabilitate the people who were displaced by the Kaptai dam. As a result, for their life and subsistence, a big portion of the tribal people have moved to the adjacent states of India and Burma. (Most of those who went to India were coaxed back by the Government or were not welcome there.)

Above all, the people are deeply concerned about the afforestation programme of another 81 mouzas.

For the above reasons, great pressure has been created on the cultivable land and this problem has been made more acute by the land grabbing by people from neighboring districts. Because of the backwardness and weakness of the tribal people, there was once a law prevalent in the country since the British days not to grant settlement or land to outsiders. But it is a matter of great regret that since the days of partition, though the hill tracts regulation is still in force, due to the weakness of the administrative machinery or their wilful negligence, this rule has not been enforced. For this reason, within a short time, a large portion of the Feni Valley, which was mostly inhabited by the hill people, has been completely occupied by people from other areas. Similarly, the rich valleys of Bandarban have also been taken over.

Being unable to protest, the tribal people now fear that they might become completely uprooted. All hillsmen think of Bengal as their mother, of Bengalis as their brothers, and of themselves as the youngest son. Each and every inhabitant of the hills thinks of the hills as the breasts of his mother. This mother's breast is most dear to him. This child is not prepared to share this breast with his elders. As you are the elder ones, you have the power and intelligence to take it by force, but we have no intention to allow you to touch it. This is our last word. We consider this to be the main problem of the CHT.

Honourable President,

If you consider it to be a problem at all, the solution is as follows:

1 The flow of illegal infiltration should be stopped immediately.

2 After appropriate inquiry, the persons who have acquired settlement illegally and had land transferred to themselves should be properly dealt with.

3 The existing regulation on land administration, with its sections and sub-sections, should be effectively enforced.

In addition, we also submit the following related proposals:

1 All the cultivable land in the reserved forests should be given for settlement.

2 The water level of Kaptai lake should go down to its lowest level from the first week of February.

3 This level should be maintained until the end of August.

4 The system of agricultural loans should be simplified, with provision for both short and long-term loans.

5 In the recently rehabilitated area of Marishya, one hospital with the necessary equipment should be erected.

For the improvement of communication in the CHT, we present the following proposals:

1 An all-weather road from Rangamati to Mahalchari and Khagrachari.

2 A similar road from Rangamati, via Chandraghona, to Bandarban.

3 The two roads from Khagrachari to Panchari and from Khagrachari to Dighinala should be metalled.

4 The rehabilitated zone of Bagaichari Police Station should be developed with the construction of roads.

Though the Karnaphuli hydro-electric project provides electricity for the overall needs of the country, it is a matter of great regret that except for the neighbouring Chandraghona and Rangamati areas, there is no electricity in other parts of the region.

Another problem is irrigation. If the Agricultural Development Corporation would supply lighter power pumps at reasonable rent, then the agricultural produce could be increased several times. At the same time, if the Government could supply power tillers, the possibility of producing agricultural products could be doubled.

The above proposals are not exhaustive. To accelerate the development programmes, we propose to set up one permanent development board through which the different developing programmes could be made, examined and implemented, and completed in time.

(The last part of the memorandum, which follows, is considerably abbreviated.)

Due to mismanagement on the part of the Government, the corruption of officials and the opportunism of cliques, the people live in a state of anguish. We implore that a committee be sent to verify the situation.

There should be administrative corrections:

1   To help the District Commissioner, one powerful advisory committee should be formed with representatives from the tribal people.

2   The police force should be drawn from the tribal people, and placed under the command of the Deputy Commissioner (in order to minimize abuse, and for faster redress when it occurs).

Appendix 6
The Bangladeshi Intervention, Geneva 1983

Intervention by Mr Alimul Haque, First Secretary, Bangladesh Mission, Geneva, before the Working Group on Indigenous People on 12th August, 1983, in reply to a statement by The Anti-Slavery Society, London

Mr. Chairman,

We have asked for the floor to refer, by of some preliminary remarks, to a document submitted to this Working group by the Anti-Slavery Society of Great Britain. I take the floor, Sir, more in pain than in anger, because the document purports to be a report on the "Indigenous people" in Bangladesh. It is painful because we have to be told by foreigners that there is a segment in our population, which must be categorised as indigenous populations.

Sir,

It is the understanding of my delegation that the present proceedings of the Working Group on Indigenous people are devoted to an objective and non-polemical study for the evolution of standards concerning the rights of Indigenous people worldwide. On the other hand, the format of the so-called report on so-called Indigenous people in my country is cast in the form of a complaint and a judgement, breath-taking in its impertinance. It cannot be seen as a *bon-fide* contribution to a scientific study aimed at achieving the primary objective of this working group, namely the evolution of standards concerning the rights of Indigenous peoples.

In the first place the report begs an important questions namely the definition of Indigenous people. While we understand that the question of definition of Indigenous people is by no means settled, it is the submission of my delegation that the paradigm situation must be derived from the historical experience of countries in the western Hemisphere and in Australasia where a colonising and racially distinct people coming from overseas established settlements and entered into a situation of conflict with the autocthon population of those countries. It will be evident that the situation in no part of Bangladesh conforms to such a paradigm. The Bengali speaking majority of Bangladesh has been settled in this area since pre-historic times and have co-existed through recorded history with tribal peoples in an area which is half the size of Federal Republic of Germany. In other words the entire population of Bangladesh may be described as autocthon without straining language. If, therefore, fundamental conceptions are not to be compromised, reports such as the one submitted by the Anti-Slavery Society should be expunged or at least treated with the utmost reserve.

Mr. Chairman,

My delegation submits that it is not possible to understand the basic thrust of the Anti-Slavery Society's document without reference to the legal and constitutional framework that obtained specifically in colonial times. As this working group is no doubt aware, the Government of India Act of 1935 provided for a separate dispensation for the so-called tribal areas in the scheme for the Governance of British India. I quote below section II of chapter I of part two, entitled the Federation of India:

"The functions of the Governor-General with respect to defence and ecclesiastical affairs and in respect of external affairs, except the relations between the Federation and any part of His Majesty's dominions, shall be exercised by him in his discretion, and his functions in, or in relation to, the tribal areas shall be similarly exercised".

The administration and disposition in the tribal areas were thus left to the discretion of the Governor-General i.e. the representative of British Crown, and by definition not to an elected official. The system of criminal justice was also separate from that obtaining in the rest of British India. Certain basic provision of the Criminal Procedure Code and the Indian Evidence Act were not extended to the tribal areas. There is evidence to suggest that the colonial authorities regarded the tribal areas as sensitive security areas inhabited, according to them, by wild and barbarous people to whom the benefits of a civilised system of administration and of justice could not be extended without jeopardy. The majority of the tribal areas, including Chittagong Hill Tracts, were close to or adjacent to the frontiers of British India, and considerations of a geo-political nature conditioned the entire attitude of the colonial power. There have never been as such any indigenous people on the soil of Bangladesh. The entire population of the territory which now comprise Bangladesh has always been and still is one people – Bangladesh nation. It was also the policy of the colonial authorities to isolate the tribal areas and to deny them the benefits of modern communications, agricultural and industrial development, education and health care.

On the emergence of Bangladesh into independence, the separation of the Chittagong Hill Tracts as a tribal area was rejected politically as well as legally. These former tribal areas were brought into the mainstream of Bangladesh life. Their representatives stood for, and were elected to local as well as national legislative bodies. Cabinet Ministers were appointed from these tribes and in every way the paternal colonial dispensation terminated. An attempt has also be made to bring the fruits of economic development to the inhabitants of these areas through capital investment in roads, housing, hospitals, post offices and schools. The Bangladesh constitution guarantees equal access to the laws as well as to economic opportunity irrespective of the residence or of the tribal affiliation of its citizens. It has been alleged by the Anti-Slavery Society that there is evidence of economic degradation in the Chittagong Hill Tracts. It is the submission of my delegation that such degradation and economic deprivation that there is, is shared by the 96 million people of Bangladesh. The economic situation of my country is well known to the International Community. We are a country enjoying per capita income of 120 US dollar per year. The people of Bangladesh have to share the available resources in an equitable manner within the severe economic constraints well-known to the international community.

The Anti-Slavery Society has recommended that an "influx of Bengali settlers" in the Chittagong Hill Tracts must be halted. Mr. Chairman, when there is no influx, how can we stop it? Moreover, Bangladesh is a country with a homogenous people. People of one area may like to travel to another area. How can we deny our citizen the right to travel from one part of their own country to another? We therefore, cannot understand what has been meant by the expression "Bengali settlers" by the Anti-Slavery Society. We the people of Bangladesh are all Bangladeshis. The question of one group of Bangladeshis travelling to another part of their own country do not become settlers. Mr. Chairman, reference has been made to an expansion of the administrative and police machinery in the Chittagong Hill Tracts by the Anti-slavery Society. Mr. Chairman, all that my Government has done in this area of the country is to assist the people in the area to undertake improvement in their economic activities for development. These include better use of fallow land, extension of agricultural services, road building, health, sanitation and population planning. There has been no visible opposition to government assistance from the people of this area, just as there has been no opposition to similar activities by government in any other area of the country. There has naturally been an expansion in the administrative machinery of the government in this area, just as there has been a similar expansion in the rest of the country, commensurate with the Governments policy of accelerated socio-economic development of Bangladesh. The people in the Chittagong Hill Tracts enjoy equal opportunities in all spheres of life with the rest of the nation, and the same protection of law. Peace and communal harmony prevails in all part of Bangladesh including the Chittagong Hill Tracts. An allegation has also been made that 100,000 troops have been stationed in the area. Those who are familiar with Bangladesh will know from the figure quoted alone that the allegation is without foundation.

The Anti-Slavery Society also purports to monitor the accession of sovereign states to various international instrument and to make far-reaching recommendations about special missions under United Nations auspices to visit my country. There are number of bodies such as the

Committee on the Elimination of Racial Discrimination and others that have been entrusted with the responsibility of monitoring accession, ratification and application of a number of international instruments of the United Nations. It is not part of the functions of the Working Group or of any NGO to duplicate these efforts and dissipate scarce resources on work that distracts from its main task. Thus, these irrelevancies, apart from being an expensive distraction, many we submit, compromise the viability of the Group's substantive work.

Finally my delegation would like to submit to you that a major portion of the work of the Working Group needs to be devoted to an indepth study of the colonial past in third world countries in order to deepen its understanding and insight into the present historical situation. If the working group agreed on this much-needed study, my delegation is prepared to pledge its unstinted support in order to arrive a balanced historical picture of the present situation in various parts of the world. Indeed it is ironic that NGO's that are playing a praisewarthy role in the economic development of many countries, many of which are based in former colonial powers, have not thought of looking at the colonial record in some depth. They are well placed to do this. An objective chronicle of the colonial past, would, I submit, be a valuable contribution to the work of this Working Group.

My delegation reserves the right to revert to this matter at a later stage, should it be necessary.

Dated: Friday 12th August, 1983

Glossary

ADB Asian Development Bank. An international funding agency, Japanese-dominated and with its headquarters in Manila, the Philippines.
ADAB Australian Development Assistance Bureau. The official aid agency of the Australian government.
Awami League Sheikh Mujib's secular political party. It won the 1970 Pakistani election on a platform of autonomy for East Pakistan.

Circle A revenue-collecting area in the hill tracts; three were confirmed by the 1900 Regulation.

Dao Broad-bladed knife traditionally used in the Chittagong Hill Tracts.
Dewan The (usually hereditary) leader of a goza.

GOC General Officer Commanding; an especially powerful position under martial law.
Goza A Chakma kinship group.

Joutha Khamars Co-operative farming schemes forced on tribespeople by the Dhaka authorities; they came into being after the flooding caused by the Kaptai dam.
Jhum The hill tracts term for a forest clearing where tribespeople grow subsistence crops. The plot is made ready by the method of slash and burn. After harvesting, the cultivators move on to clear another patch. This system, also known as shifting or swidden cultivation, allows constant soil regeneration, but demands large areas of forest.

Karbari The traditional leader of a hill tracts village.

Lakh One hundred thousand (100,000).

Mound A unit of weight; approximately 82 lbs.
Mouza The smallest administrative unit (a number of villages) for tax collection in the hill tracts recognised under the 1900 Regulation.
Mukti Bahini The guerrillas of the Bangladeshi army in operation during the 1971 war.

Panchayat A low-level assembly; originally a village meeting.
Police Station This can also mean a thana, a unit of administration between a union and a sub-division.

Rakki Bahini A para-military force raised by the Sheikh Mujib government to enforce its policies.

Seer A unit of weight; approximately 2 lbs.

Shanti Bahini The armed fighters drawn from the hill tracts tribes; literally, Peace Force.

SIDA The Swedish International Development Authority. The official aid agency of the Swedish government.

Thana See police station.

The 1900 Regulation The common form of the Chittagong Hill Tracts Regulation, 1900. This provided for a limited form of selfgovernment by the hillmen during the British raj.

UNICEF United Nations International Children's Fund.

USAID United States Agency for International Development. The official funding agency of the United States government.

Union Council A union council is a sub-section of a thana; there are 47 of them in the hill tracts.

WHO The United Nations World Health Organization.

Note Transliteration has led to variations in the spellings of hill tracts names. Thus Karnaphuli is sometimes Karnafuli, and Khagrachari is sometimes Khagrachhari. The Tripura tribe is also called Tippera or Tipra (some anthropologists include the Tripuras in the Kuki group). The Marma peoples are also known as the Moghs but, as this means river pirates, it is considered derogatory. The Chakmas call Chittagong, Chadignang, and Kaokhali, Kobakhali. Throughout this report the commonest or easiest spellings have been adhered to.

Key Dates

1666 Chittagong Hill Tracts annexed by Mughals.

1757 Battle of Plessey.

1760 Under agreement with the Nawab, Mir Kashem Ali, Bengal seceded to East India Company.

1785 Chakma Raja Jan Bux Khan recognised British hegemony in the tracts.

1860 British administration of the hill tracts began; appointment of a Superintendant of the Chittagong Hill Tracts.

1881 Creation of three administrative circles in tracts.

1898 Administrative headquarters for the district moved to Rangamati.

1900 The Chittagong Hill Tracts Regulation gave special status to the area and the 13 tribes were allowed jurisdiction under their own chiefs and headmen.

1921 Chittagong Hill Tracts declared "backward area" by Britain.

1935 Hill tracts declared "totally excluded area" by Britain.

1947 Pakistan and India independent from Britain; the hill tracts included in East Pakistan.

1959 Basic Democracies Order replaced the indigenous political system.

1962 New constitution of Pakistan; colonization of hill tracts began.

1963 Kaptai dam completed displacing 10,000, mostly Chakma, families.

1964 Special status of hill tracts abolished.

1970 Awami League wins majority in Pakistani National Assembly elections.

1971 Bangladeshi Provisional Government declared in Calcutta; civil war begins.

1972 Constitution of newly formed Bangladesh promulgated; abrogation of Chittagong Hill Tracts Regulation of 1900.

1975 Assassination of Sheikh Mujib; Major-General Ziaur Rahman became Chief Martial Law Administrator.

1980 Massacre at Kaokhali bazar of 300 tribespeople.

1981 Disturbed Areas Bill passed, allowing police and army to shoot anyone suspected of anti-state activities; massacre of an estimated 500 tribespeople at Matiranga; Ziaur Rahman assassinated.

1982 Lieutenant-General Mohammed Ershad becomes Chief Martial Law Administrator.

1983 Ershad declared himself President; amnesty offered to tribal resistance force, the Shanti Bahini.

Bibliography

Agrar Hydrotechnik GMBH in association with Halcrow Fox and Associates, *Chittagong Hill Tracts Development Project,* July 1978.

Anti-Slavery Society, "Genocide in Bangladesh", *Anti-Slavery Reporter,* December 1981.

Asian Development Bank, *Reconnaissance Mission to the Chittagong Hill Tracts, Bangladesh,* May 1976.

Bangladesh Institute of Development Studies, *Population in Forestry Communities Practising Shifting Cultivation: a Case Study of Bangladesh,* October 1979.

Centre for Social Studies, Dhaka University, *Chittagong Hill Tracts: a Socio-Economic Monograph,* April 1978.

Chittagong Hill Tracts Development Board, *Annual Report,* 1979-80.

Choudhury, R I et al, *Tribal leadership and Political Integration,* University of Chittagong, 1979.

Forestal Forestry and Engineering International Ltd., *Chittagong Hill Tracts, Soil and Land Use Survey,* report, 1967.

Government of Bangladesh, *Bangladesh District Gazeteers (Chittagong Hill Tracts),* 1975.
District Census Reports, (various years).

Huq, M M, *Government Institutions and Underdevelopment: a Study of the Tribal Peoples of the Chittagong Hill Tracts, Bangladesh,* Institute of Local Government Studies, University of Birmingham, December 1982.

International Work Group for Indigenous Affairs, "Bangladesh: Tribals Fight for Land in Chittagong Hill Tracts", *IWGIA Newsletter,* No 27, June 1981.

Mey, Wolfgang, *Genocide in Bangladesh: the Chittagong Hill Tracts,* paper presented to 7th European Conference on Modern South Asian Studies, London, 7 to 11 July 1981.
The Chittagong Hill Tracts Case: Genocide in Context, paper presented to International Conference on Development Strategies and Social Resistance in the Third World, University of Copenhagen, April 1983.

United Nations, Commission on Human Rights, Sub-Commission on Prevention of Discrimination and Protection of Minorities, *Summary of Information Relating to Bangladesh,* Study of the Problem of Discrimination against Indigenous Populations: special rapporteur, Mr. José Martinez Cobo.

Zaman, M Q, *Tribal Integrity and National Integration: the Chittagong Hill Tracts Case,* paper prepared for seminar on Tribal Cultures of Bangladesh, University of Rajshahi, 28 to 30 March 1980.

The Chittagong Hill Tracts
Militarization, Oppression and the hill tribes

This report has been sent to:

the President of Bangladesh
the High Commissioner for Bangladesh, London
the United Nations Centre for Human Rights, Geneva
the International Labour Office, Geneva and London
the World Bank, Washington
the Asian Development Bank, Manila
the European Commission of Human Rights, Strasbourg
the Commonwealth Secretariat, London
the Foreign and Commonwealth Office, London
the British-Bangladesh All-Party Parliamentary Group, London
the Parliamentary Human Rights Group, London

and was presented to the Working Group on Indigenous
Populations of the United Nations Human Rights Commission
in Geneva in August 1984.

**The Anti-Slavery Society for the Protection of Human Rights calls on these
organizations and individuals to act within their competence to ensure that
peace and justice prevail in the Chittagong Hill Tracts of Bangladesh.**

If you are concerned about the issues raised in this report, contact the
Anti-Slavery Society,
180 Brixton Road,
London SW9 6AT

and the
Bangladesh International Action Group,
2a Brewery Road,
London N7

Anti-Slavery Society Reports

Indigenous Peoples and Development Series

Report No. 1
The Philippines – authoritarian government, multinationals and ancestral lands
189 pages. 1983. ISBN 0 900918 14 4
£2.50 (US $5).

This and other Anti-Slavery Society Reports are available from:
Third World Publications,
151 Stratford Road,
Birmingham B11 1RD.
Telephone 021-773 6572 and 01-607 4463

Cheques payable to Third World Publications

The Anti-Slavery Society
for the Protection of Human Rights

Our aims are in accordance with the principles of the Universal Declaration of Human Rights, 1948.

They are:

1   The elimination of all forms of slavery including forced labour.
2   The defence of the interests of both oppressed and threatened indigenous peoples.
3   The promotion of human rights in accordance with the principles of the Universal Declaration of Human Rights, 1948, and of the International Covenants on Civil and Political Rights and on Economic, Social and Cultural Rights.

If you are in sympathy with these aims, please join the Society.

Application Form

To
The Director,
Anti-Slavery Society,
180 Brixton Road, London S W9 6AT

I have much pleasure in contributing to the funds of **The Anti-Slavery Society for the Protection of Human Rights** the sum of .... pounds and .... pence per annum and wish to be enrolled as a member.

Name ....

Address ....

....

....

Subscriptions

An Annual Subscription of £10 and upwards will constitute the subscriber a Member of the Society (Canada and U.S.A. 20 dollars).

An Annual Subscription of £3 will constitute the subscriber an Associate Member of the Society.

Life membership is offered on payment of £125 (Canada and U.S.A. 250 dollars).

A Bankers Order Form is printed overleaf.

Members paying income tax in the United Kingdom, and agreeing to subscribe by Deed of Covenant for four years enable the Society to recover the tax due to the Inland Revenue at no extra cost to the subscriber. (Deed of Covenant printed overleaf.)

Note: We find that the legal wording confuses some subscribers and makes difficult their completion of the Deed. If you wish to give the Society £10 p.a. please complete the form as follows: "... net yearly sum of £10." The Society, as a registered charity, is allowed to claim from the Commissioners of Inland Revenue a refund of the income tax at the current rate already paid by you on the sum covenanted.

Deed of Covenant

I, ...
of ....
hereby Covenant with the Anti-Slavery Society for the Protection of Human Rights
of 180 Brixton Road, London SW9 6AT, that during the period of four years from
the date hereof or during my life, whichever is the shorter period, I will pay to the
Treasurer for the time being of the said Society for the general use of the Society,
such sum as will, after deduction of income tax, leave in the hands of the Society

the net sum of .... such sum to be paid annually, the first payment
to be made on the .... day of .... 19....

Dated this .... day of .... 19....

.... (Signature)

Signed, Sealed and Delivered by the above-named in the presence of

Signature of Witness ....
Address ....
....
Occupation ....

Banker's Order

To Messrs. ....
Please pay to Barclays Bank Ltd., 463 Brixton Road, London SW9 8HL, to the
credit of the **Anti-Slavery Society for the Protection of Human Rights,** the sum of
£.............. on .... and on .... in every
succeeding year until otherwise ordered.

Signature ....
Address ....
....

£   p

This form, signed by the subscriber, should be forwarded to the Director of the
Society.

Cheques and postal orders should be made payable to the Anti-Slavery Society.

96